# Connecting Policy to Practice in the Human Services

# Connecting Policy to Practice in the Human Services

## Brian Wharf and Brad McKenzie

OXFORD
UNIVERSITY PRESS

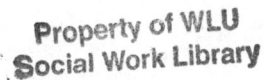

# OXFORD
UNIVERSITY PRESS

70 Wynford Drive, Don Mills, Ontario M3C 1J9
www.oupcan.com

Oxford University Press is a department of the University of Oxford.
It furthers the University's objective of excellence in research, scholarship,
and education by publishing worldwide in

Oxford  New York

Athens  Auckland  Bangkok  Bogotá  Buenos Aires  Calcutta
Cape Town  Chennai  Dar es Salaam  Delhi  Florence  Hong Kong  Istanbul
Karachi  Kuala Lumpur  Madrid  Melbourne  Mexico City  Mumbai
Nairobi  Paris  São Paulo  Singapore  Taipei  Tokyo  Toronto  Warsaw

with associated companies in Berlin  Ibadan

Oxford is a trade mark of Oxford University Press
in the UK and in certain other countries

Published in Canada
by Oxford University Press

Copyright © Oxford University Press Canada 1998

The moral rights of the author have been asserted

Database right Oxford University Press (maker)

First published 1998

Canadian Cataloguing in Publication Data

Main entry under author:

Wharf, Brian
Connecting policy to practice in the human services
Includes bibliographical references and index.

ISBN 0-19-541413-6

1. Canada – Social policy. 2. Social planning – Canada. I. McKenzie,
B.D. (Bradley Douglas). II. Title.

HN107.W533 1998    361.6'1'0971    C98-931503-7

Cover & Text Design: Max Gabriel Izod

2 3 4 -  02 01 00

This book is printed on permanent (acid-free) paper ∞.
Printed in Canada

# Contents

## Part Two
## Toward an Inclusive Paradigm in Policy-Making

# Acknowledgements

Since the primary audience for this book is students, it is appropriate that we begin by acknowledging the help provided by students at the Universities of Victoria and Manitoba. Earlier drafts of the manuscript were used in the multidisciplinary graduate program at the University of Victoria and in the graduate program of the Faculty of Social Work, University of Manitoba. Accustomed to the experience of having their papers critiqued, students revelled in the opportunity to turn the tables by pointing to inconsistencies in the material, to the failure to document claims and arguments, and, for the Victoria students, the chance to identify 'murky' sentences—a comment that often appeared on their papers! The names of the students are listed below.

Particular thanks go to Karen Potts at the University of Victoria who gathered together the comments of her classmates, added her own insights, and wrote a perceptive review of the manuscript. Glenn Stalker, a research assistant for Brad McKenzie, also reviewed the manuscript and made helpful suggestions on content. Linda Campbell reviewed the chapter on policy analysis and provided useful feedback on this material.

Thanks also go to Professors Kathy Teghtsoonian and Michael Prince at the University of Victoria who used the manuscript in two policy/practice classes and contributed many helpful comments.

As is always the case, a heavy share of the responsibility for inputting and collating the material fell to our secretaries—Claudette Cormier (University of Manitoba) and Barbara Egan (University of Victoria). We thank them for fitting the manuscript into their busy schedules.

At Oxford University Press, Euan White was enthusiastic about the book from the beginning and Jane McNulty improved the final version with some deft editing. We thank, too, the anonymous reviewer who made some helpful observations. We have attended to most if not all of the reviewer's concerns.

Finally, we wish to pay tribute to our wives. Marilyn Callahan provided her usual astute advice to Brian and continues to enliven his days. Madeline McKenzie reviewed drafts of several chapters and provided Brad with encouragement and support throughout the project.

## University of Victoria: Class of 1995
Barbara Field, Sarah Glass, Brian Hill, Douglas Hillian, Maureen Hobbes, Angela Leski, Norma McLelland, Madeleine Mills, Karen Potts, Janet Rankin, Georgia Rendle, Camille Roberts, Annette Schultz, Vicky Scott, Vaida Siga, Charlette (Sam) Somers, Rona Sterling-Collins, Robina Thomas, Linda White, Leslie Woodman

**University of Victoria: Class of 1996**

Colleen Adrian, Patti Anderson, Penny Anguish, Shelley Briggs, Fiona Crisp, Iris Elsdon, Anne Field, Lauralyn Houle, Monica Jobe, Caroline Martin, Angus Monaghan, Mona Skinner, Heidi Tonn, Anne Wood

**University of Manitoba: Class of 1995**

Robert Bonnefoy, Frank Caldwell, Denise Cronin-Forsyth, Heather Ferguson, Gio Guzzi, John Hutton, Eduardo Mendarozqueta, Mary Cox-Millar, Karen Mitchell, Geoff Ripat, David Scott, Carrie Solmundson, Chris Sunde

# Preface

Our interest in a more participatory approach to policy-making comes from several sources. First, our experience in direct practice, even if it was many years ago, taught us an early lesson: the policy directives from head office seldom responded adequately to the needs of service users. Even when well-intentioned, it seemed that policy-makers just couldn't 'get it right'. We were convinced then that front-line practitioners, working more collaboratively with service users, could make an important contribution to the policy-making process, and although often frustrating, our early experiences in trying to influence the policy-making process reinforced this view. Even in our current roles—that involve teaching about policy-making and contributing to policy development through consultation and evaluation—we remain convinced of the importance of new, more inclusive forms of practice and their ability to respond in meaningful ways to the needs of service users. While improvements to practice may occur in the absence of a more participatory approach to policy-making, these are much more likely to happen if a framework that includes practitioners and service users in both policy-making and implementation processes is adopted.

Second, our teaching in this area, primarily within social work, led to the recognition of a couple of problems. On the one hand, some students failed to see the relevance of devoting much time to understanding policy and the policy-making process. They argued that most of the important policy decisions were made by government and that they could have little influence over these decisions. Therefore, it would be more productive to concentrate on smaller practice and organizational issues because they would be more likely to be able to change these. On the other hand, students with a keen interest in policy-making found shortcomings in the existing literature. Two particular problems were identified. One was the fact that much of the literature provided a macro-level critique of social policies without identifying approaches to policy-making that might make a difference to the nature and scope of such policies. Another was the observation that in literature on the policy-making process, the focus was most often limited to a general discussion of public policy processes at the federal government level. Discussion of policy-making processes that were relevant to the human services and that could be transposed to the provincial and non-government sector were in short supply. In a very real sense, both groups of students were correct. The challenge for us was to demonstrate that policy-making was relevant to practitioners, and that there are ways to build a policy-making process that is more inclusive of both practitioners and service users. While we have tried to answer this challenge, we also recognize that these approaches are not entirely new, and that they are not easy to implement. Many of the strategies and examples identified in the book have emerged from the creative efforts of policy-makers and practitioners who have struggled with this very issue, and we have tried to summarize both the benefits and the shortcomings of these efforts.

Our third motivation arises from observations about recent changes in the policy-making environment. A market-driven economy, both globally and domestically, is 'all the rage' these days, and in this context it is difficult to build support for progressive social policies. Governments on the right and on the left are intent on balancing their books, and in February 1998 the federal government announced its first balanced budget in approximately three decades. In a policy environment characterized by cutbacks, the rhetoric of decentralization and community partnerships is often used to promote offloading and obscure centralized control over key decision-making processes. The prospect of surplus operating revenues has already raised new questions about whether to replace some of the cuts to social spending, whether to pay down the debt, or whether to reduce taxes. In this context, a new debate is emerging and there is significant public support for increased social and health care spending. In addition, an increased reliance on community partnerships and non-government organizations provides opportunities to do things a little differently even if certain risks must also be recognized. In this new era, policy-making in the human services will take on a new level of importance at the federal, provincial, and organizational levels.

The book is organized in two parts. Part 1 lays the groundwork for new approaches by outlining models of policy-making and the policy-making process. The introductory chapter identifies some of the problems of policy-making within the human services. Chapter 2 explores definitions of policy, who makes policy, and the policy-making context. Chapters 3 through 6 examine various models and stages of the policy-making process. Throughout Part 1, we focus attention on the gap between policy and practice, and on the challenge of building a policy process that includes the expertise of practitioners and service users. A key aspect of the policy-making process is policy analysis, and a model for policy analysis is presented in Chapter 5. An example of policy analysis utilizing this model was developed by Karen Campbell, a former student, and this is included as an Appendix (p.135) in the book.

Part 2 contains four chapters that identify participatory models of policy-making and assess the potential of building a more inclusive paradigm for policy-making in the human services. Two of these chapters are case studies; this is consistent with our theme of building on knowledge rooted in practice. Chapter 7, written by Stephen Owen, outlines a model for shared decision-making. While this model is based on experiences gained in resource management, the principles and issues raised are relevant to the human services. In the second case study, authored by Deborah Rutman in Chapter 8, the experience of a policy community's role in the development of guardianship legislation is described. Chapter 9 explores the theme of community governance and its potential to promote a more inclusive approach to policy-making. Chapter 10 ponders the question: How do we begin to incorporate more inclusive approaches to policy-making in the current human services policy environment?

*Brad McKenzie and Brian Wharf*
*March 1998*

# Notes on Contributors

**Brian Wharf** is Professor Emeritus, Faculty of Human and Social Development, University of Victoria. During his career at this university he has been Director of the School of Social Work, Dean of the Faculty of Human and Social Development, Professor in the multidisciplinary policy-practice program, and Acting Director of the School of Public Administration. He is the author/editor of numerous books, including *Community Organizing: Canadian Experiences* (Oxford University Press, 1997) and *Rethinking Child Welfare in Canada* (McClelland and Stewart, 1993).

**Brad McKenzie**, Ph.D., is Associate Professor at the Faculty of Social Work, University of Manitoba, where he teaches in social policy, program evaluation, and child welfare. He has done extensive research in the field of child welfare, particularly in relation to First Nations child and family services, and was Anglophone Editor of the *Canadian Social Work Review* from 1996 to 1998. Publications include *Current Perspectives on Foster Family Care for Children and Youth* (Wall and Emerson, 1994).

**Stephen Owen** is the Lam Professor of Law and Public Policy and the Director of the Institute for Dispute Resolution at the University of Victoria. He is also a Commissioner of the Law Commission of Canada. Professor Owen has previously been the Deputy Attorney General, Commissioner of Resources and Environment, Ombudsman, and Executive Director of the Legal Services Society of British Columbia.

**Deborah Rutman**, Ph.D., has been a Senior Research Associate with the School of Social Work/Faculty of Human and Social Development, University of Victoria, since 1991 and the Director of the Child, Family and Community Research Program since its inception in 1994. Deborah's recent and current research activities include: the experiences and support needs of families affected by Fetal Alcohol Syndrome/Effects; the development of alternative policies for pregnant women who misuse substances during pregnancy; community development and collaborative approaches to service planning and delivery; and adult guardianship.

**Karen Campbell** completed her chapter when she was a student in the Master of Social Work Program at the University of Manitoba in 1996–7. She is completing her thesis on casinos as economic development in Aboriginal communities using Casino Rama in Ontario as a case study. She currently lives in Ottawa where she is doing social policy research and analysis for the federal NDP caucus.

**Part 1**

## Policy-Making and the Lack of Inclusiveness in the Human Services

# 1
## Introduction

The primary audience for this book is students in human service programs. We also hope that the book will be of use to practitioners and to recipients of human services. Our intent is threefold: to introduce students to traditional ways of policy-making and to critique these methods; to argue that policy should be built from practice; and to suggest some inclusive structures for policy-making. Building policy from practice requires finding ways to incorporate into the policy-making process the knowledge not only of practitioners but also of the people they serve. Including practice-based wisdom will require changes in the structures and approaches to policy-making that currently characterize the process. In addition to these organizational reforms, we advocate new and inclusive approaches to policy-making—such as shared decision-making, policy communities, and community governance—that will provide opportunities for everyone involved, including citizens at large, to participate.

We are well aware that the changes we suggest will not be welcomed by the key players in the policy-making process. Since our proposed changes would involve more people, these changes will be seen as hampering an already often lengthy and complex process. Our rejoinder to this criticism is that the involvement of those affected is not only a principle we respect, but current approaches have not achieved the goal of improving the human condition. To exclude the wisdom of practitioners and those affected by the policy-making process will simply extend this record of failure.

We are also aware that certain language usage can actually hinder effective communication and with this in mind, we have tried to limit the use of professional jargon, whether it stems from policy-makers or from practitioners. In addition, we identify some language that, while in common usage, stigmatizes those who receive services. One example among many is to refer to these individuals as 'cases' and to professionals as 'case managers'. In our view, the usual labels of 'client', 'patient', 'case', and even 'consumer' are demeaning and inappropriate and we have discarded them. As much as possible, we refer to 'clients' as individuals or people who receive services (i.e., service users) or as those with whom professionals work. Although the phrasing may seem clumsy on first reading, our intent is to replace demeaning labels with respectful language. While we regard the term 'consumer' as the least objectionable of these labels, we have tried to minimize the use of this term as well.

Given our audience of students, practitioners, and individuals who receive services, it seems appropriate to begin the book with a story from practice. The story involves a project that challenged child welfare workers to change child welfare practice (Callahan and Lumb, 1995). During a meeting a worker commented that she and her co-workers were 'stressed out' because of the demands of new legislation, required training programs, a new computer system, and increasing workloads. Indeed, she noted that no less than five workers were currently on stress leave. When she finished speaking, a single-parent member of the group exploded. *'You're* stressed out—what a bunch of crap! You have a well-paying job, a nice house and furniture, a car and holidays, and you probably have a husband and kids at home. I have nothing—no job, I'm on welfare, my kids have been taken away by you lot and you think you have problems!'

The group sat in silence for awhile as the young woman cried and then tried to compose herself. The co-ordinator of the project asked her if she would like the group to get involved in her struggles. The woman nodded and in a most supportive manner the other single parents began to ask questions: Why had her children been apprehended? Why was she on welfare? To some answers they nodded understanding. To others they indicated that their experiences differed and based on these experiences they proffered suggestions for action. For example, one woman noted that she had relied initially on her child welfare worker to develop plans but that she had decided eventually that this reliance was inappropriate and insufficient. She had assumed some leadership, therefore, and had suggested specific steps she could take related to employment and counselling. To her surprise she found the worker receptive, and together they developed plans designed to ensure the return of her children.

The lessons from this example are not new to those steeped in and committed to group work and mutual aid: the lived experience of the single-parent women in the group made their questions and their suggestions legitimate and respectful. Hence, their support was well received. Parenthetically, we might add that the entire event was completely new and therefore disconcerting to some child welfare workers who were used to working with people on a one-to-one basis.

The key question raised by this example is: if this strategy works in practice—if people being served can contribute to the resolution of issues—why can't the same process work in policy? As will become apparent throughout this book, however, traditional approaches to policy-making ignore the wisdom of practitioners and of those being served. Indeed, our biggest complaint regarding current policy processes is that at all stages they exclude those who are most affected by the outcomes of the process. In a very real sense, policies are initiated, planned, and implemented by people who will be unaffected by the programs or services. Some examples include policies for First Nations people, for children who are neglected and abused, for the unemployed and the poor, for the elderly who are poor, and for people with disabilities (although some changes are evident for the latter group). Only in the last-remaining universal policy arenas of health and education do policy-makers and providers have a stake in the outcomes of their work, but even here some escape avenues can be found in private schools, nursing homes, and medical clinics.

In attempting to unravel this dilemma we must acknowledge that policy-makers, legislators, and senior bureaucrats are usually men, while practitioners who implement policy and those who receive services are usually women (Wharf and Callahan, 1984). Indeed, the predominantly male policy-makers are also middle-aged and prosperous; and while some may have begun their careers as practitioners, others have never experienced the stresses and challenges faced in practice. In addition, and even more importantly, most policy-makers have grown up in and continue to live in comfortable, middle- or upper-class homes and have only the faintest empathy for the poverty-ridden lives of those who receive services. Hence, the knowledge and experience gap between those who make policy and those who must live with the consequences is enormous.

A second step in the unravelling process can be found by examining the organizational structure of government. The fundamental premise of representative democratic government at the provincial level is that authority is rooted in the premier's office, in Cabinet, and in the legislature. Thus, a minister is in charge of his/her ministry and all actions are undertaken in the minister's name. In order to ensure that this occurs, governments have established hierarchical organizations in which authority is delegated from the minister to a deputy minister, to associate or assistant deputies, to regional directors and, finally, to the staff who actually carry out the legislation and the policies. And as ministries have grown in size and complexity, so has the challenge of ensuring compliance with the will of the legislature.

This approach to organizing work has become known as the corporate style of management. Whether intended or not, this style has effectively divided practitioners and their immediate supervisors from senior managers and policy-makers. It has resulted in the 'industrialization of social work practice' (Fabricant, 1985), whereby practitioners are stripped of their professional judgement and discretion and are expected to conform to a highly routinized work environment.

Another way of understanding the corporate style of management is afforded by the analysis of Kouzes and Mico (1979). These authors identified three domains within organizations: *policy, management,* and *practice*. The policy domain is occupied by politicians and senior bureaucrats such as deputy ministers. The primary concern of this domain is to develop policies and programs that will enhance the image of the political party in power. Will new programs or the elimination of existing programs win the favour of the electorate? On the other hand, practitioners are dedicated to their profession, to its standards, and to the needs of those with whom they work. The combination of these pressures often results in a demand for more resources and improved services. For its part the management domain is caught in the middle, trying to assure the policy-makers that programs are being efficiently run while at the same time responding to the demands of practitioners for additional resources.

The differences among these three domains can become so large that 'the result of the interactions of these domains is an organization that is internally disjunctive and discordant' (Kouzes and Mico, 1979, p. 456). However, it is important to add that this analysis, while helpful, does not include those receiving services. To add this fourth domain would strengthen the claim that public sector organizations are severely flawed.

We should emphasize that we hold a view that is not widely shared. We believe that those we serve can make valuable contributions in identifying the circumstances that make their lives difficult and in pointing to ways of overcoming these difficulties. This view sets us apart from those who hold that professionals have the knowledge and skill to both identify problems and to prescribe solutions. It also sets us apart from those who advocate that the remedies to today's problems lie in a return to patterns of the past; for example, women should return to home and hearth, divorce should be made more difficult, and voluntary agencies and the church should assume an expanded role in social services. For those who hold these neoconservative views, it is not particularly important to find ways of including the excluded: if service users cannot take care of their own affairs, it is argued, they can scarcely contribute to the complex business of planning and governing programs.

Here is the conundrum: while on the one hand we believe in including the excluded in policy-making, human service professionals are employed by organizations that not only exclude those who receive services from participation but also transform them from 'citizens' into 'clients'. In a very real way, public sector human service agencies, organized in a hierarchical fashion and enmeshed by rules and regulations, are part of the problem. A vexing dilemma associated with the innovative approaches described in Part 2 is how to include and to give weight to the opinions of those who have traditionally been excluded. The research on citizen participation is voluminous and unanimous in the conclusion that only the 'well off, the well spoken and the well educated' participate (Wharf Higgins, 1997).

It is important to recognize that service users do not participate for some practical reasons: they are busy people; usually they do not receive a welcoming or personal invitation to participate; and for them, the meetings are boring and held in inconvenient locations at inconvenient times. In addition, they do not participate because they do not feel they have the right to do so—they feel like second-class citizens who have nothing to contribute. Hence, while the practical issues related to meetings can be resolved, the pervasive feeling of being a second-class citizen is much more difficult to address.

The concept of 'citizen' in Western democracies seems to be reserved for those who are working, earning a wage, and thus paying their way, or for those who have worked or are deserving of help for clearly recognizable reasons; for example, the elderly or people with disabilities. The feeling of loss of citizenship is experienced most acutely by those who are unemployed and who are dependent on society for a living. This is no wonder, since as a society we are at our meanest when it comes to dealing with the long-term unemployed, with street youth, with single mothers, and with those addicted to alcohol or drugs.

In a classic text on community action, Marris and Rein highlight the issue in the following fashion:

> The dilemma of community change arises whenever the restoration of individual dignity is taken as a psychological problem inherent in those who are demoralized, rather than as a moral problem inherent in the society which demoralizes them. We derive our sense of worth from the whole context of relationships which define a social being. To restore dignity we must above all treat people with respect. The poor need the respect of employers, nurses, social workers, policemen and public officials. And this means not only politeness but an honesty of purpose which does not disguise the shortcomings of the services offered. (Marris and Rein, 1967, p. 189)

Treating people with respect applies to the policy-making process, to the management of agencies, and to practice. It is a view that replaces suspicion with trust. It replaces regulations to be obeyed and inspection of these regulations, with support and a valuing of first-line practitioners. This view is identified by writers such as Peters and Waterman (1982), Brodtrick (1991), and Mintzberg (1983). While practised in a few business organizations, it is rarely found in the public sector.

An intriguing example of this view comes from the voluntary sector. Gary MacCarthy, a former long-time director of the Vancouver United Way, claims that one of the characteristics of successful United Way organizations is that they value and support their member agencies. Should an agency experience problems either in management or in service delivery, the United Way will offer assistance to overcome the problem. The essential point is that the agency is seen as having a problem and not as a 'problem agency'. According to McCarthy, less successful United Way organizations treat their member agencies with suspicion, believing that they are mismanaged or that there is an excessive duplication of services.

Replacing suspicion with respect at all levels of the human service enterprise is a challenge we have yet to meet. Writers such as John McKnight have advocated the creation of caring communities where networks of support provide a context for relationships that enhance self-worth (McKnight, 1995). Research by Cameron (1995), Fuchs (1995), and Callahan and Wharf (1995) has demonstrated the efficacy of social support networks in neighbourhoods and among single-parent women.

The concept of the caring community has much to commend it. But if caring stops at the community level, if it is taken to mean that nothing beyond the boundaries of the community matters, then communities can become closed. To use Montgomery's phrase, they can become subject to 'acute localitis' whereby an élite controls the affairs of the community (Montgomery, 1979). Even more importantly, acute localitis can lead to values and behaviours characterized by prejudice and fear. The gated communities now becoming popular in the United States provide an apt example of this point.

Hierarchically organized structures and corporate management practices continue to dominate the public sector, and only occasionally do some signs of change become evident. These are hesitant signs for which there is as yet no firm commitment. They represent interesting innovations rather than established directions.

To conclude this introductory chapter, we emphasize again that our vision of the policy-making process is one that includes those affected as important contributors; that is characterized by an attitude of respect and that requires new roles for professionals at all levels of the process.

# 2

## Policy: What Is It and Who Makes It?

### What Is Policy?

The three objectives of this chapter are to outline our understanding of what policy is, to identify who makes policy, and to describe general characteristics of the policy-making environment. The first step is to come to grips with an understanding of just what social policy is. Some definitions are both abstract and all-encompassing. Thus, MacBeath defines social policy as the 'right ordering of relationships between men and women who live together in society' (MacBeath, 1957, p. 3). Similarly, Gil views social policies as 'guiding principles for ways of life, motivated by basic and perceived human needs' (Gil, 1990, p. 23). According to these views, social policy is synonymous with public policy and encompasses all of the actions of governments in their continuing but not always consistent attempts to regulate social and economic structures and citizens' quality of life.

The distinction between *grand* and *ordinary* issues is useful in clarifying the meaning of social policy. Grand issues are those pertaining to the fundamental structure of political and economic life. These grand issues include those on the distribution of income and wealth, on the distribution of political power, and on corporate prerogatives (Lindblom, 1979, p. 523).

The *grand issues* are dealt with on a national and, increasingly, on a multinational level. They represent the major economic and fiscal challenges that confront all levels of government but particularly the federal government. While many social commentators have argued that the challenges should have the well-being of all citizens as their primary concern, the reality is that economic and fiscal matters take precedence in Canada. The prevailing assumption is that if the economy flourishes, then all will benefit and the resources will be available for social and health programs.

To a certain extent this assumption is valid. Certainly all citizens benefit from full employment and a healthy economic climate. But if the grand issues are dealt with by exporting jobs to other countries with lower rates of pay, by eliminating jobs, by a regressive income tax structure, and by a failure to develop and retain adequate and universally available programs in income security, health, and education, then many citizens are relegated to poor-paying jobs or to a life of poverty.

In contrast, the *ordinary issues* concern more personal matters, such as the provision of health and social services and planning for the development of cities and neighbourhoods. While the grand issues set the context for ordinary matters and exert considerable influence on them, there is considerable scope and slack available to policy-makers concerning the nature of services and how best to provide these services. For example, Canada has followed the lead of the United States in dealing with the grand issues involving the economy (McQuaig, 1991), but the traditional Canadian path with regard to policies for health and social services has deviated from the American model in some fundamental ways. Thus, Canada has a universal health care system, although it must be noted that this program is under considerable threat in the current social policy climate.

For most citizens on a day-to-day basis, the ordinary issues assume great significance. Given our interest in connecting the efforts of social workers and other human service practitioners with the policies that govern their practice, our focus is on the ordinary issues of social policy and we have selected the following definition as a guide:

Social policy is all about social purposes and the choices between them. These choices and the conflicts between them have continuously to be made at the governmental level, the community level and the individual level. At each level by acting or not acting, by voting or not voting, by opting in or contracting out, we can influence the direction in which choices are made. (Titmuss, 1974, p. 131)

The relevant parts of this definition are *purpose, choice,* and *level.* Policy is all about choosing directions—in situations in which choices are clouded by conflicting values and where facts and information cannot be marshalled to establish clearly that one choice is superior to all others. Thus, the term 'policy-making' is reserved here for wrestling with and deciding among various difficult choices. The choices are made at a variety of levels: for example, the federal government struggling with the thorny issue of unemployment, a provincial ministry of health plagued by uncertainties surrounding the delegation of responsibility to communities; and the dilemma facing a settlement house trying to decide if a demonstration held to protest the income assistance policies of a provincial government will jeopardize future funding.

Although the topic is not often posed in these terms, we argue that 'policy' choices also confront practitioners in their work. Should nurses working with senior citizens opt for home support or long-term care? Should child welfare workers dealing with a situation of child neglect recommend apprehension of the children or the provision of a range of support services to the family? The choices facing practitioners are just as difficult and perplexing as those that baffle policy-makers. Furthermore, these choices have to be made in a context that involves people in a highly immediate and compelling fashion and in which the consequences of the choice are of immense significance to people's lives.

It is important to emphasize that all of these struggles in policy-making and in practice are surrounded and complicated by firmly held ideologies and beliefs. Indeed, decisions are framed by ideologies and personal experience, and while research and information can complete and round out the frame, they rarely alter it to any significant extent. We deal with the notion of framing in the discussion of the initiation stage in Chapter 4 and again in Chapter 10, but we need to establish at the outset the intimate connection between ideologies and politics.

We note throughout the book that the policies of governments are suffused by partisan politics. The actions of politicians and political parties are guided by ideologies that represent firmly held views of the appropriate role for the state, and these ideologies have a significant impact on social policies. The most significant ideologies are *neoconservative*, *liberal*, *socialist*, and *Marxist*. It is of course presumptuous to present these views in a brief and condensed fashion, given that a voluminous literature exists on each, and we have no intention of trying to summarize the work of the main theorists in this area. However, it is important to recognize the general relationship between these ideologies and social policy. Table 2.1 sets out the key points of this relationship.

**Table 2.1** The Relationship Between Ideologies and Social Policy

| Ideology | Selected Proponents | Relationship to Social Policy |
|---|---|---|
| Neoconservative | Ronald Reagan<br>Margaret Thatcher<br>Preston Manning<br>Mike Harris | A residual approach based on the 'Charity Model' is advocated, reflecting the belief that social programs destroy individual initiative. Thus, social programs should be provided only as a last resort. |
| Liberal | Pierre Trudeau<br>Jean Chrétien<br>Bill Clinton | Public social programs are important in addressing general risks to well-being, but these are subservient to economic issues. |
| Democratic Socialist | J.S. Woodsworth*<br>David Lewis<br>Tommy Douglas | Advocates commitment to universal social programs and stipulates that social policy should be equal to economic policy and should be based on need. |
| Marxist | Karl Marx<br>Vladimir Ilyich Lenin<br>Mao Tse-tung | Social programs under capitalism blunt the revolutionary potential of the working class through piecemeal appeasement. Economic transformation is the key to equity and social development. |

*J.S. Woodsworth was the first leader of the federal Co-operative Commonwealth Federation (CCF), the predecessor of the New Democratic Party (NDP). David Lewis was a leader of the federal NDP. Tommy Douglas was the NDP premier of Saskatchewan at the time medicare was introduced in that province.

The differences among these political philosophies are substantial and the consequences for citizens and social programs are profound. Although they deal with equity and fairness issues in different ways, only the socialist and Marxist philosophies are centrally concerned with these issues and none address gender and racial inequalities as an overriding priority.

Policies set the context for practice in some significant ways. For example, British Columbia's Family and Child Service Act (1980), which was enacted by a neoconservative government, contained no provisions for support and preventive services. At a later point some of these services were established, but, in keeping with an overall government policy of privatization, the services were assigned to voluntary agencies. In accordance with a residual approach to child welfare, ministry staff were assigned two roles: as investigators of complaints of child neglect and abuse, and as case managers of the services provided by voluntary agencies. Missing were the long-standing social work roles of counsellor and advocate for clients. This policy has had a lasting and far from positive impact on the culture of the ministry and its reputation in communities. Indeed, the report of a community panel established to inquire into the state of child welfare in British Columbia commented that for many citizens the predominant image of child welfare workers was that of 'social cops' (Report of the Community Panel, 1992, p. 124).

A more recent example involves the preoccupation with 'bashing the poor', led by neoconservative governments in Alberta, Ontario, and Manitoba. For example, welfare benefits have been cut by 16 per cent in Alberta, and 21 per cent in Ontario.

The discussion outlined above highlights the impact of policy on practice and the need for practitioners to alter the negative effects of policies on service users, and to find better ways of connecting practice with new policies that are being developed.

## The Current Policy Environment and Who Makes Policy

In our view the grand issues of social policy are controlled primarily by a relatively few men in business and in the federal government. Often, in fact, they exchange positions, serving for a time as a politician or senior bureaucrat and then assuming responsibilities in the business world. Our view of who rules is supported by numerous studies dating back to the groundbreaking research of Porter (1965) and continuing through the work of Clement (1975 and 1983), Panitch (1977), and Newman (1975 and 1981). These studies consistently found that a relatively few men, largely of Euro-Canadian descent, have prospered under the existing structures and values of Canadian society and enjoy a disproportionate amount of influence in maintaining these structures and values. Among other matters, they control both the distribution of income through employment and the redistribution of income through the tax system. While the latter has had a very modest redistributive effect, the share of the market income of the top quintile of the Canadian population has always hovered around 42 per cent while the share of the bottom quintile has fluctuated between 2 and 3 per cent (Torjman and Battle, 1995; Kitchen et al., 1991).

The most recent and compelling accounts of who rules and in whose interests are provided in a series of best-selling books by Linda McQuaig. The series began with an examination of the tax system in Canada (*Behind Closed Doors*, 1987), followed by an inquiry into free trade and the GST (*The Quick and the Dead*, 1991). McQuaig's analysis continued with an investigation into the decline of support for health and social security programs (*The Wealthy Banker's Wife*, 1993). A more recent publication, *Shooting the Hippo* (1995), probes the reasons for the national debt. In these books some consistent themes emerge: the growth of multinational corporations, the unequal distribution of power and wealth, the unfairness of the tax system, and the declining support for health and social programs.

Recently most governments in Canada have been preoccupied with eliminating the deficit as a single-minded agenda. Public spending cuts, particularly to social programs, coupled with monetarist policies,[1] increased tax revenues, and low interest rates, led to a balanced federal budget in 1997–8. Yet the official rate of unemployment in 1997 remained between 9 and 10 per cent, with more than 1.3 million Canadians out of work. The unemployment rate among young people is particularly high, and it is well understood that the official rate of unemployment underestimates the real rate of unemployment when one accounts for discouraged workers who stop looking and part-time workers who would prefer to work full-time. Cuts to the health and social safety net threaten the very foundation of medicare, and major reductions in welfare and unemployment insurance benefits, coupled with profits in excess of $1 billion annually for some banks, illustrate the growing problem of inequality. Based on 1995 statistics, the National Council of Welfare described the growth of poverty in this way:

> Bluntly put, the modest economic growth of the last several years was simply not filtering down to the ranks of the poor . . . . Increases in poverty among families pushed the overall poverty rate to 17.4 per cent and the number of poor Canadians to a 16-year high of nearly 5.1 million. (as quoted in Galt, 1997, p. A4)

These examples demonstrate the failure of the federal and most provincial governments to respond to social objectives, including job creation, despite their pre-election commitments. And this failure is not just a question of resources. Cutbacks in social programs are currently justified on moral as well as economic grounds. Curiously, it is becoming popular to advance the view that what the poor need most is more hardship and more stigmatization, not improved opportunities, to help them rise out of poverty! Why has this argument achieved so much currency in a society with a historical commitment to the values of caring and sharing? In his populist book *Shakedown* (1996), Reid defines this change as a transition from the 'spend and share' era of the 1960s through the 1980s, to the 'sink or swim' era of the 1990s which is defined by shrinking incomes, corporate downsizing, and declining government services. While an economic boom in the stock market makes the top 20 per cent of Canadians richer, the bottom 80 per cent are getting poorer. Technology and globalization, he argues, are killing more jobs than they are creating.

Others go beyond this pessimistic description of the transformation of Canadian society and attempt to provide an explanation for current policies. For example, Teeple (1995) identifies globalization as a primary cause of this transformation in that national impediments to global market relations are undermined and dismantled by neoliberal or structural adjustment policies. The role of the state to regulate commerce, welfare, and any form of distributive justice is subjected to policies of privatization and deregulation. We need only examine the impact of free trade, not only on economic sectors but on social and cultural policy, to see evidence of this trend.

Marchak (1991) advances a similar argument based on her research of the rise of the 'new right' in the global context. The new right stands in opposition to the welfare state and in favour of completely free markets untrammelled by state intervention. She suggests that the rise of this political ideology parallels the failure of the state to provide social services free of debt even though Canada's debt is primarily attributed to causes other than social spending. In this vein Cameron and Finn (1996) have noted that government spending on social services since the 1970s has been responsible for only about 6 per cent of the federal debt. Moreover, Canada spends less on social programs compared to thirteen other developed countries, including Greece and Spain, and social spending, at present, is growing more slowly compared to all other spending in the economy. Despite these trends, the presence of a high public debt has led to an increased demand to privatize public programs, including the social services.

In addition, the new right articulates the concerns of a great many people. It must be recognized that ideology does not exist independently from people's lives; rather, daily life reflects and shapes one's ideological commitments. Citizens are faced with rising taxes, declining incomes, poorer services, the past failures of social programs, and a rising debt—all of which reinforce the ideology of the new right. For example, it has been argued that the federal government's 1997 budget, which continue to reduce federal government commitments to social spending for the poor, was inspired by a series of polls that demonstrated a hardening of public attitudes toward those earning low incomes (Owen, 1997, pp. A1–2).

A related issue is that of transnational corporations, which supersede the welfare state in many instances. Having grown from 7,000 twenty years ago to 40,000 today, transnational corporations control 33 per cent of the world's assets while employing only 5 per cent of the world's work force (Council of Canadians, 1997, p. 11). The state is increasingly unable to regulate the activities and tax the surplus of globalized capital, and if the Multilateral Agreement on Investment (MAI) is approved, this will extend the global power of corporations to an unprecedented level. While negotiations failed to meet an April 1998 deadline, the MAI remains a priority for members of

## Box 2.1 Corporate Tax Evasion

In 1994, 81,462 corporations made $17.1 billion in profit but paid no corporate taxes. Eighty per cent of the $17.1 billion of untaxed profits was earned by corporations making more than $1 million in profits in 1994, and 46 per cent of these untaxed profits was earned by corporations making more than $25 million in profits in 1994. The finance sector which includes banks, trust, and insurance companies accounted for nearly one third of the corporate profits that went untaxed and in the past two years untaxed profits in this sector exceeded $5 billion.

Source: Canadian Centre for Policy Alternatives (1997). *The 1997 Alternate Federal Budget Framework in Brief.*

the Organization for Economic Cooperation and Development (OECD), a group of the twenty-nine richest countries in the world. The MAI is designed to ease the movement of capital across international boundaries. Among other provisions, the MAI would prevent preferential treatment of local or domestic firms, ban rules requiring foreign companies to invest in the local economy, ban any restrictions on the repatriation of profits and capital, and give multinational corporations the right to sue governments who might try to enact laws to protect their local or national economy. Under this agreement, threats of plant shutdowns and relocation to other countries, repeatedly used by corporations to extract extraordinary benefits from the state, would become that much easier to implement. The diminished power of the state in these matters parallels the loss of power that labour has experienced in dealing with such corporations; thus, the development of globalization is likely to lead to increasing conflict between labour and capital.

Two possible scenarios related to diminished State power are identified by Marchak, although others may exist. First, decreasing State power may lead to the mobilization of actions to promote policy reform on a more global scale. One example of this is the movement to curtail forced child labour spearheaded by Craig Kielburger, a young activist from Thornhill, Ontario, who runs a group called 'Free the Children' (Morris, 1995). A second possibility is that social policy will adapt to an environment characterized by a diminished state role, particularly with respect to the State's capacity to regulate the national economy. If the latter scenario prevails, we will become increasingly less able to rely on government to protect the health and social programs we have come to value in Canada.

Strategies to address these national and international issues are beyond the scope of this book. However, policy-making in the health and social service sector today cannot ignore broader questions about the Canadian political economy. And it is not simply a matter of learning to accept less. Three arguments support a much more proactive stance. First, public concerns about issues such as health care, child welfare, and child poverty will have a significant impact in shaping future policies in these areas. For example, concerns about child poverty have remained on the policy agenda of the federal government because of public and interest group advocacy, despite the government's woefully inadequate efforts to deal with this pressing social problem. Advocacy and social action groups have an important role to play in supporting these policy directions. For example, an alternative federal budget was developed in 1997 and 1998 by a coalition of groups co-ordinated by the Canadian Centre for Policy Alternatives and Choices, a Winnipeg-based group committed to social justice. These proposals demonstrate how the federal budget could be used more effectively to create jobs and improve social programs while incorporating an ongoing commitment to deficit reduction. Also, smaller-scale policy initiatives make a difference to the people served by these policies, while providing program models or options that can contribute to larger and more comprehensive changes. Initially, shelters for abused women were developed on a very small scale, but a network of these resources now spans the country. Finally, governments play an important role in facilitating new and potentially beneficial policies even in times characterized by political and fiscal conservatism, and progressive policy-making is all about how to influence and shape more of these kinds of policies. For example, in 1995 the Conservative government of Manitoba initiated 'For the Sake of the Children', a three-hour educational program for divorcing and separating parents. Based in Winnipeg, this early-intervention pilot project received government funds for an external evaluation. On the basis of the evaluation completed during the pilot phase, the program has been expanded to six hours in duration and extended to other regions of the province.

One aspect of élite rule is that élites are so confident of their position that they seldom bother to challenge the analyses of new critics. Indeed, they have not only camouflaged their privileged position, but have also convinced Canadians that spending on social programs is responsible for the deficit. Contrary and compelling evidence for the fallacy of the claim that the debt was caused by spending on social programs comes from none other than Statistics Canada's own journal, the *Canadian Economic Observer*. 'It was not explosive growth in program spending that caused the increase in the deficit after 1975 but a drop in federal revenues relative to the growth in the Gross National Product . . . and the biggest drop was in the amount paid by corporate taxes' (Mimato and Cross, 1991; see also Box 2.1). An interesting footnote to this study is provided in McQuaig's *Shooting the Hippo* (1995). She reports that the accuracy of these conclusions was verified by a number of reliable sources, including staff of the Economic Council of Canada, but they were a source of embarrassment to senior officials within the Ministry of Finance. The finance department was determined to cast blame for the deficit on excessive spending on social programs and wanted to turn a blind eye to evidence that diminished this claim. In response the associate deputy minister of finance ordered Statistics Canada to repudiate and retract the study's findings. While Statistics Canada did not go this far, the August 1991 issue of the *Canadian Economic Observer* included a mild disclaimer that regretted any inconvenience the article may have caused (McQuaig, 1995, p. 62).

The same attitudes are evident in the actions of corporations and business firms that lay off workers in the interests of increasing efficiency and profits and then expect social programs such as unemployment insurance and social assistance to assume responsibility for providing financial support to these workers. To compound the irony, business leaders then criticize social programs for being too generous and for being responsible for the deficit. Yet the excessive remuneration paid to business executives is, in that community, a cause for celebration. Each year *The Globe and Mail* publishes the salaries (including other compensation components such as stock options) for the top one hundred Chief Executive Officers (CEOs) of Canadian companies. In 1997, fifty CEOs made between $2.0 million and $27.4 million, and another fifty made between $909,467 and $1.9 million (*The Globe and Mail*, 1998, 18 April, pp. B6–B7). At the top of the heap in 1997 was Robert Gratton, president and CEO of Power Financial Corp., and in the entire list there is not one woman. Most CEOs posted raises well over 100 per cent and many were between 200 and 700 per cent.

We should note here that the findings of studies of power at the national level in Canada are paralleled by similar studies in the United States (among others in a voluminous literature, see Mills, 1959; Domhoff, 1967 and 1971; Lundberg, 1968; and Lapham, 1988). The conclusions of these studies are summarized in a book excerpt that appeared in *Harpers Magazine*:

> . . . the people who run big business bear a remarkable resemblance to the people who run big labour, who in turn might be mistaken for the people in charge of the media and the universities. They are the same people. . . . Almost exclusively white, disproportionately mainline Protestant or Jewish, most of the members of the American élite went to a dozen Ivy League colleges or top state universities.
>
> . . . Not only do the comfortable members of the overclass single out the weakest and least influential of their fellow citizens as the cause of all their sorrows, but they routinely and preposterously treat the genuine pathologies of the ghetto—high levels of violence and illegitimacy—as the major problems facing a country with uncontrollable trade and fiscal deficits, a low savings rate, an obsolete military strategy, an anachronistic and corrupt electoral system, the worst system of primary education in the First World and the bulk of its population facing long-term economic decline. (Lind, 1995, p. 38)

While we have summarized information supporting the influential role played by élites in society, there are dissenting voices. One interesting challenge to the position that the élite rule in their own interests, without any counterbalancing of their power, is provided by a series of case studies of policy communities in Canada. These case studies are collected in a book that examines the influence of policy communities on public policies (Coleman and Skogstad, 1990). The case studies and the conclusions are interesting not only because they suggest some modifications to the élite view of power, but also because they provide some useful information on policy communities. We deal with the latter in Chapter 8, but we comment below on the conclusions about the exercise of power.

The case studies examine a number of policy communities including the East Coast fisheries, farming communities in Ontario and Quebec, the banking industry, forestry, the women's movement, the poverty community, the occupational health industry in Quebec, and labour. All the cases consider the extent to which policy communities influence or alter the autonomy and the capacity of the state. 'Autonomy' is defined as the ability to act in an independent fashion, while 'capacity' refers to the ability of the state to marshal the resources it requires to translate its intentions into outcomes.

Following their analysis of the case studies, the editors come to the following conclusions:

> We reject the societal-centred argument that public policy is a function of the preferences and influence of social forces or interest groups and that state officials or institutions have little autonomy to shape public policy in their own vision. Equally we do not accept that characteristics of the state alone—its institutional structures and/or the capacities and goals of political officials within it—can explain policy outcome. Rather, explanatory import is enhanced by examining closely the interaction between state and societal actors. (Coleman and Skogstad, 1990, pp. 313–14)

The editors reach this conclusion about the interaction between state and societal actions in the exercise of power and influence despite the fact that the case studies dealing with the two least-developed and weakest communities—the women's movement and the poverty community—reveal quite clearly that these groups have had little impact on the social policies of the federal government. On the other hand, and as one might expect, the policy communities in banking and forestry did influence the actions of government, and it is no accident that the memberships of these policy communities consist primarily of wealthy and influential individuals. This reinforces rather than weakens our argument that élites exercise a disproportionate amount of influence in Canadian society, particularly in relation to the grand issues of public policy.

Since the grand policies established at the international and national levels set the overall direction for Canadian society and determine the resources for health and social programs, examining who rules at the provincial and local levels may seem relatively unimportant. Yet the consequences of grand policies affect people in their local communities—on their streets, playgrounds, schools, and workplaces.

Despite the pervasive influence of the grand issues and the limited mandate of local governments, these and other local governing structures do have an important part to play. For example, the policies of school boards and of individual schools shape and influence the quality of education in communities. Similarly, the actions of municipal governments with respect to land use, social planning, recreation, and neighbourhood organizations affect a number of important services, and in many provinces the emergence of district health boards will play a major role in determining the quality of health care. While we recognize that grand policies are very significant in determining the overall issues of power and income distribution, we are primarily concerned with the ordinary issues of social policy. For example, we are concerned with who makes policy in child welfare and how the products of this process affect the lives of children.

There are few detailed analyses of the structures of power at the provincial and municipal levels in Canada. Earlier decades in the United States saw a veritable spate of case studies following the publication of *Community Power Structure* (Hunter, 1963). This study concluded that a small élite group of businessmen effectively controlled the big decisions in the city of Atlanta, Georgia. Other studies came to different conclusions. Thus, the analysis of who participated in a number of significant decisions affecting life in New Haven, Connecticut revealed that the issue determined who was involved: those who participated in decisions concerning education did not carry any influence in other public matters (Dahl, 1961). In addition, the New Haven study revealed the pervasive influence of a dynamic mayor and city council. And a later study of Atlanta disputed Hunter's findings and, like Dahl, concluded that pluralism rather than élitism characterized decision-making (Jennings, 1964).

Essentially, the conclusions of the 'who rules?' studies at the community level fell into two camps: the pluralist explanation typified by *Who Governs?* (Dahl, 1961) versus rule by a small group of élites as exemplified by *Community Power Structure* (Hunter, 1963). The debate between those advancing the pluralist versus the power élite positions revealed significant differences in the methodologies used to obtain information in support of their position. For example, inquiries that asked 'Who are the most important individuals in town?' did indeed elicit names of prominent citizens. Conversely, studies that traced the ebb and flow of particular policies not infrequently revealed that a large number of citizens, not necessarily all from the upper class, were involved in making decisions about schools, hospitals, and other local matters. Evidence also emerged to support the conclusion that power structures differed from city to city, and among communities at different stages of development.

While the debate concerning methodological issues raged fiercely for a time, it did not change a significant factor common to both camps. Regardless of how many members of power groups were involved, the 'who' were male, middle-class, professional, and/or businessmen. Relatively few women, poor people, and members of ethnic minorities took part in the decisions that affected them. Although the membership of women has increased, significant participation by other groups is absent from local governing structures.

A related body of literature on the participation of citizens in the governance of health, education, recreation, and social services agencies supports the above-noted conclusions. Again, the research is largely US-based, but some Canadian studies exist as well. The consistent conclusion is that opening up opportunities for participation usually results in these opportunities being seized by professionals and middle-class citizens. Thus, a study of participants in the community resources boards established by an NDP government in British Columbia in the mid-1970s revealed that 44 per cent were directly employed in the human services; 18 per cent were lawyers and businessmen; 14 per cent came from the trades and clerical sector, and retired citizens and housewives predominated in the remaining 34 per cent (Clague et al., 1985).[2] Low-income citizens and users of services were noticeable by their absence. Similarly, when child welfare services were decentralized to six agencies governed by community boards in Winnipeg in 1985, the boards were dominated by white, middle-class professionals.

In fact, this finding should come as no surprise. In the first place, individuals receiving services are busy people struggling to eke out an existence with inadequate incomes, and they often move frequently in search of employment or because of low incomes. Ironically, their busy lives are created in part because of the complicated pattern of human service agencies. Most service users do not own their own cars and have to travel by public transit from agency to agency, each having its own intake and service requirements. In the second place, most of us accept invitations to participate in a group only if the invitation interests us, if we believe that we can make a difference, and if we think we will be welcomed by and will feel comfortable with the people issuing the invitation. To date, human service organizations have failed to address all of these necessary aspects of participation.

A recent study of citizen participation in the New Directions health reform in British Columbia confirms the above observations. After noting that members of low-income, disability, and other marginalized groups were conspicuous by their absence, Wharf Higgins contacted these groups and asked whether they were uninterested in health issues and why they had not accepted the invitation to participate. The responses are illuminating:

> Their experiences suggest that as a result of circumstances beyond their control—a mental illness, a physical disability, the inability to live at home, their ethnicity—their rights as a citizen in society had gradually, systematically been stripped away. Validation as a taxpayer, a person, a citizen had expired. The First Nations groups spoke of their long history with colonization and the mistrust of government. The single parents and youths referred to the medical community's disdainful treatment of them as patients. (Wharf Higgins, 1997, p. 290)

We return to some of the conclusions and recommendations of this study in Chapter 9.

Within health and social service organizations the pattern of governance is repeated. Health policies are set by physicians and administrators who are usually men, and these policies are implemented by nurses, social workers, physiotherapists, and speech therapists, most of whom are women. In the social services, men have assumed most of the policy-making roles, and women have assumed most of the responsibility for implementation (see Callahan, 1993; Swift, 1995a and 1995b). In our view, this unequal distribution of power is detrimental to the overall purpose and outcomes of child welfare and other fields in the health and social services. The consequences of this inequality, and some possible ways to change this distribution of power, are explored in subsequent chapters.

# 3

## Policy-Making Models and
## Their Connection to Practice

### Generic Policy-Making Models

In attempting to provide a short list of policy-making models relevant to the social services, we face a formidable task. First, as noted in the previous chapter, the policy environment at a provincial, national, and, more recently, global level plays a significant role in policy development. This environment is shaped by ideological, technical, and socioeconomic variables that have a major impact on such factors as the amount of resources governments are prepared to commit to new policy initiatives, particularly in the health and social service sectors; moreover, the influence of these variables is difficult to predict and to incorporate into any model. Second, the arena or level within which policy-making occurs can influence the nature of the process. For example, somewhat different models or approaches may be adopted by an organization concerned about the number of adolescent offenders being identified in its catchment area compared to the models adopted by a federal government concerned with social security reform. Finally, policy-making in practice remains difficult to classify because each situation is unique and the process is adapted, to some extent at least, to that particular situation. For example, one important variable is the exercise of power related to the political process, and the relative importance of politics varies considerably from one situation to another.

The policy-making process outlined in this chapter includes an introduction to five different models. Three commonly identified approaches are the *rational* or *synoptic approach*, *incrementalism*, and *mixed scanning*. These models are frequently referred to in the literature; in effect, they have stood the test of time, although each has its limitations. A fourth, which can be referred to as the *value criteria model*, incorporates values as a more explicit component of the policy-making process. This model is an adaptation of the rational model and was developed by the Institute for the Study of Child and Family Policy at North Carolina (Dobelstein, 1990; Moroney, 1991). In fact, Rein (1970) and Titmuss (1968) can be identified as early advocates of the need for explicitly including value criteria as a component of the policy-making process in the human services.

A final model summarized in this chapter is an adaptation of the *'garbage can' model* originally coined by Cohen, March, and Olsen (1972) in their study of universities, and later adapted by Kingdon (1995) to explain how policies are developed at the governmental level. This model recognizes the importance of both problems and solutions as major ingredients in the policy-making process; however, it also explicitly recognizes the central role of politics, a somewhat neglected attribute of other models. This model places more emphasis on the actual process of policy-making and can be used to explain why, in the real world, good plans don't always get adopted. We have selected these models for inclusion because they can be adapted to planning and policy-making at both the organizational and governmental levels. The characteristics of each of these models are identified below.

### The Rational Model

The rational or synoptic approach is based almost entirely on the analysis of objective data in an orderly sequence. This approach to policy-making is anchored in systems theory and the analysis of factual or observable data using the scientific method. While the irrationality of the policy process may be acknowledged, proponents of this model are more likely to attribute this irrationality to the unwarranted interference of politics, politicians and political agendas. The preferred role for the planner is that of the expert technician who co-ordinates the complex tasks associated with policy-making. The development of the rational model is often associated with Herbert Simon, a consultant with the Rand Corporation during the 1950s, and its popularity with the government of the United States coincided with the appointment of Robert MacNamara as the Secretary of Defense in John F. Kennedy's administration in the early 1960s. Fresh from his success as the Chief Executive Officer of the Ford Motor Company, MacNamara was determined to transfer business techniques to the public policy field. Analytical tools such as benefit-cost analysis and program policy budgeting systems (PPBS) were adopted. Both reflected a goal-oriented approach to policy development in which goals and measurable objectives would be clearly identified, and options would be evaluated in monetarized benefit-cost ratios. The synoptic or comprehensive rational model features five general steps (Carley, 1980):

1. Define the problem in objective (behavioural) terms and classify general goals.
2. Develop a list of all feasible alternatives that would resolve the problem under prescribed circumstances.
3. Project the general consequences that are likely to flow from each strategy and the probability of those consequences occurring.
4. Examine data appropriate to each alternative and determine the relationship of predicted outcomes to goals and objectives and the relative benefit-cost ratio of each alternative strategy.
5. Select a strategy that best approximates identified goals and objectives or that achieves the best benefit-cost ratio.

Several problems have been identified with the rational model. One is the difficulty of identifying and analysing all feasible alternatives in determining the single best solution. In social policy development, this can be characterized as an information- or knowledge-related problem in that most policy decisions involve situations or circumstances that are somewhat unique; the consequences cannot be adequately predicted; and only a limited number of variables can be considered (Moroney, 1991). A second issue is the question of values. While a comprehensive rational model may incorporate value considerations, the assumption is that once values are clarified, they can be ranked and dealt with in the same ways as other types of information. In effect, the policy-maker is assumed to play a neutral or value-free role. Thus, policy-making within the rational model stresses technical rationality where the focus is on examining the most efficient means to achieve a predetermined end. The problem is, however, that the relative merits of these ends are given inadequate attention, and we are often left with policies that may work on technical grounds but which are none the less 'bad policies'. The classic example of the Holocaust and the role of Nazi officers in carrying out policy is frequently cited as exemplifying this problem. Finally, the rational model often assumes that implementation follows logically from policy-making; thus, it frequently pays inadequate attention to the implementation phase of policy development.

While the comprehensive rational model is associated with an analysis of all possible alternatives, this criterion was later modified by suggesting that the analysis stage could be concluded once a satisfactory alternative was located. The result was policy development within a framework of 'limited rationality'. While this modification may address questions of feasibility in applying the model, it also sacrifices some of the appeal of arriving at the most desirable policy choice following a more comprehensive search for alternatives. A major problem with either the limited or more comprehensive rational approach is the lack of attention to values or to whether the 'ends' of policies can be justified. A new policy may be designed to carry out a stated goal efficiently and effectively; however, with insufficient attention to whether the predefined goal provides a valued benefit and for whom, a rational model of policy-making may be used to promote the adoption of undesirable policies. Even if this result is unintended, a more limited form of rational planning may be likely to encourage decision-makers to evaluate alternatives according to their own values because they remain in complete control of the process.

Despite these limitations, the rational model—or some of its major aspects—is widely applied in practice. It is reflected in the medical model and in many of the planned-change models adopted in the human services. These approaches stress an orderly process of change beginning with assessment or diagnosis, followed by goal selection. The professional is cast in the role of the expert or change agent working *on* rather than *with* a patient or client, who is conceived as a largely passive recipient of services.

In social policy sectors such as child welfare, policy development often begins with a data collection phase. The complexity of problems facing policy-makers is such that they feel overwhelmed. In some cases, task forces, Royal Commissions, or special inquiries will be mandated to outline a policy direction after gathering information, hearing from stakeholders, and initiating special studies. These strategies reflect a rational approach to policy development, and such groups can perform a useful role in policy-making in some circumstances. (See Box 3.1 for an example of a rational approach to legislative change). However, the appointment of such bodies by governments or other decision-makers can also be used as a method to avoid taking action on controversial, complex, or costly issues while appearing to give these matters serious attention.

### Incrementalism

If the rational model of policy-making can be criticized for being too isolated from the realities of practice, incrementalism has been criticized for being too closely associated with existing organizational and service prerogatives. Incrementalism is commonly associated with Charles Lindblom (1959, 1968, and 1979), who referred to the process as 'the science of muddling through'. Lindblom argued that change is most likely to occur when one calculates the marginal benefits of small adaptations from current approaches. Advocates of incrementalism suggest several benefits. First, small-scale changes avoid major disruptions and the possibility of unanticipated negative outcomes resulting from large-scale changes. For example, if a small change results in positive effects, it can be accelerated; if it leads to adverse effects, it can be halted and reversed without causing major problems. Second, incremental changes can usually be incorporated within existing organizational arrangements. Third, the approach accounts for political and normative realities by incorporating these considerations into discussions of alternatives during the change process. Furthermore, such discussions can include the views of those who make policy, those who implement it, and those who are affected by it. While incrementalism may often reflect the reality of policy implementation from the point of view of practitioners, it can be criticized for failing to consider the broader context of issues. Boulding captures the point neatly: 'We stagger through history like a drunk putting one disjointed incremental foot after another' (Boulding, 1964, p. 931).

Incrementalism generally accepts the legitimacy of existing structures and service mandates, including the existing power structure within service organizations. Thus, it adopts an essentially conservative approach to change (see Box 3.2 for an example of an incremental approach to legislative change). Although it does allow for larger-scale changes under circumstances in which marginal changes are clearly undesirable, 'muddling through' is not a preferred strategy, particularly in situations requiring significant policy change.

**Box 3.1** New Child Welfare Legislation in BC: A Rational Approach to Policy-Making

By late 1991 a number of factors converged to produce the required impetus for major change to British Columbia's child welfare legislation. These included increased criticism of the reliance on statutory authority within the 1980 Family and Child Service Act; the election of a new NDP government that espoused a commitment to more family support services and a willingness to consult with the public; and the death of an adolescent in a government-funded youth facility that led to a highly critical report from the provincial ombudsman. The government appointed a community panel composed of a mix of government and community members, and Aboriginal members formed a separate Aboriginal panel that held hearings in Aboriginal communities. These panels consulted widely; they held public meetings, received written briefs, conducted research, organized several day-long round-table discussions on special topics, and met with professional groups and organizations. This comprehensive rational approach to policy-making included a strong commitment to public participation. For example, the main panel heard 550 presentations in more than 23 communities and received over 600 briefs from individuals and groups. A broad approach to examining the needs of children and families was taken, and issues such as poverty, service integration, and the adversarial relationship between child welfare agencies and families were addressed. After several months, two major panel reports were published, each outlining broad recommendations for new legislation and a new, more preventive approach to dealing with communities, families, and children. Many of the more radical recommendations of the panel reports—such as the inclusion of a provision stating that no child would be apprehended due to a lack of family resources—were rejected. Nevertheless, the reports were accepted by the ministry as a framework for drafting the new legislation. A Legislative Review Group was appointed to draft legislation, and in the spring of 1993 an Implementation Steering Committee was formed to begin preparing the various regions for change. The Legislative Review Group consulted with a variety of groups, including regional staff, and in 1993 a White Paper, *Making Changes: Next Steps*, was released. Work continued on developing a policy paper to outline proposed legislation and this paper was approved by Cabinet in December, 1993. Under the guidance of a new minister, drafting of the new Act was completed in the spring of 1994. In June, 1994 the legislature passed the new Child, Family and Community Service Act, and its companion legislation, the Child, Youth and Family Advocacy Act.

Source: Adapted from Durie and Armitage, 1996.

**Box 3.2** Legislative Reform in Manitoba: Incrementalism in Action

In the summer of 1996 the Manitoba government launched a process to update its 1985 Child and Family Services Act. However, a very limited approach to reform was undertaken. The public consultation process was limited to a mere few weeks' duration, with only a few presentation dates in approximately six centres throughout the province. Furthermore, presenters were directed to confine their recommendations to a series of specific and quite limited policy questions published in a 'consultation workbook'. These included questions such as whether grandparents should have a right to apply for access to children who are apprehended, whether birth parents under eighteen should be able to consent to private adoption, whether private practitioners arranging for adoptions should be licensed, whether teenaged dads should be required to pay child support, and whether child welfare workers should be required to have a minimum level of training. No comments on larger issues related to the general orientation of existing legislation or problems in the current service delivery system were invited. While presenters at public hearings did not necessarily confine themselves to this narrow set of questions, their views on broader policy issues were not included in the final report published by the panel. The report of the panel then made recommendations on these issues to the minister, and some of these recommendations were incorporated as amendments to the Act in the spring of 1997. However, these relatively minor changes did not alter the general thrust or philosophy of the existing Act.

### Mixed Scanning

Mixed scanning was advanced by Etzioni (1967 and 1976) as a model that attempted to integrate the best aspects of the rational and incremental models. By incorporating a contingency approach to planning, mixed scanning suggests that situational factors will determine when each approach should be emphasized. As well, mixed scanning advocates an approach to policy development that begins with a more comprehensive scan of the existing policy, including problem analysis and alternatives, and then adopts a more incremental approach to the implementation of new policies.

Mixed scanning is a cumbersome term for a model that probably comes closest to capturing the reality of the policy-making process. Much about implementation and operational-level planning reflects an incremental approach, yet more comprehensive approaches, including the use of task forces and commissions, attest to the influence of the rational model and an attempt to scan the broad policy environment for more comprehensive solutions.

There are a number of similarities between mixed scanning at a macro level and strategic planning,[1] which has been widely adopted within human service organizations at the agency and operational level of planning over the past ten years. Strategic planning, generally oriented to developing policies over a mid-range time frame (three to five years), features the following general steps:

a)  identify historical events related to the policy context;
b)  complete a situational assessment of the internal and external policy environment;
c)  identify key issues or problems;
d)  identify options to address key issues;
e)  select the option that best reflects policy goals and incorporates results from the situational assessment phase; and
f)  assess feasibility and implementation issues (Bryson, 1988).

The process is intended to be participatory and it frequently involves board members, senior staff, and representatives from service units. Value considerations emerge through a reliance on the involvement of key organizational participants, and detailed service data or research may be used as a basis for assessing policy options and feasibility. Strategic planning is an important adaptation of general policy-making models primarily because of its potential application to agency-level policy development.

While strategic planning has been a popular approach to policy-making at the organizational level, it requires continued organizational investment to realize potential benefits. It is also plagued by two of the difficulties associated with many forms of policy-making: it is difficult to predict consequences, particularly in a policy environment where so much lies outside the effective control of specific organizations; and, most importantly, service users and front-line staff are frequently excluded from or underrepresented in the planning process.

### The Value Criteria Model

There are different versions of the value criteria model (sometimes referred to as the value-analytic model) (see Gallagher and Haskins, 1984), but they are similar in their overall approach to policy-making. First, the problem is defined and available alternatives for dealing with it are identified. While responses to a problem may represent only a limited range of alternatives, the problem analysis stage can direct the planner to key normative elements of the problem, including causality. In turn, this understanding helps to identify an adequate range of alternatives. For example, recognition of the role of the conventional child welfare system in separating First Nations children from their families, communities, and culture and the negative consequences associated with this reflect a problem statement that leads to a consideration of alternatives such as First Nations control over child welfare services, the development of more community-based foster care resources, and the development of more culturally sensitive services.

A second step is the development of value criteria for evaluating alternatives. These value criteria should reflect both a subjective and an objective understanding of the problem, and may include both universal and selective criteria. *Universal criteria* may represent comparatively general value considerations such as equity, efficiency, and feasibility, whereas *selective criteria* represent those values that are more specific to the problem or issue being considered. In the example above concerning First Nations child welfare, selective criteria may include self-determination, community responsibility, and cultural appropriateness. The third step involves the gathering of data required to assess each alternative, and the analysis of each alternative relative to benefit-cost issues and value criteria. Thus, alternatives are considered from both a normative and an economic feasibility standpoint. In the final step, the alternative that maximizes the greatest number of values, including efficiency, is recommended or a range of alternatives with identified strengths and weaknesses are discussed.

While this model has considerable appeal to policy development in the human services because of its explicit consideration of values, it is apparent that conflicts can arise over the criteria that ought to guide final policy selection. For example, if a particular policy choice maximizes more of the selected values but also requires higher costs, how is this conflict to be resolved? And who sets the key values to be used in policy selection—the decision-maker, the policy researcher, the service user, or others?

The selection of value criteria is the most controversial stage of this policy model but it should be recognized that other policy-making models incorporate values even if this is done implicitly. In the criteria-based model, values are explicitly identified; thus, at the very least, they become more visible and open to debate. While the selection of value criteria depends on the nature of the policy being considered, we regard this step as the point at which one establishes an ethical framework for policy-making. Therefore, it is important to identify guidelines for the development of value criteria. Saleebey (1990) has identified some broad philosophical cornerstones relevant to policy-making in the human services. These are: (a) beginning with an ethic of indignation about the denial of human dignity and opportunities; (b) incorporating humane inquiry and understanding based on dialogue; (c) a focus on compassion and caring; and (d) a quest for social justice. These four cornerstones foster empowerment and social change to promote equity.

In a discussion of criteria for theory evaluation in social work research, Witkin and Gottschalk (1988) arrive at similar conclusions. As adapted to our purposes, the steps in developing valve criteria for policy-making are:

a) the approach should be explicitly critical in considering historical, cultural, political, and economic factors;
b) people must be recognized as active agents in shaping as well as reacting to their environment;
c) the life experiences of social users must be considered; and
d) solutions should promote social justice.

The term 'social justice' is frequently evoked, yet it is open to various interpretations. We adopt the position advanced by Rawls (1971), who argued persuasively that social and economic inequalities created in society should be adjusted to provide the greatest benefit to the least advantaged. Social justice, then, is about redressing problems of inequality.

Box 3.3 provides an example of how value criteria have been used to shape policy development in a First Nations child and family services agency.

### The Garbage Can Model

The modified garbage can model of policy-making developed by Kingdon (1995, pp. 86–8) represents an attempt to describe policy-making as it unfolds in the day-to-day life of governments and organizations. As expected, this description points to a process that is less rational than any of the previously identified models. Three 'families' of processes are observed to exist in setting governmental agendas: *problems*, *policies*, and *politics*. These are likened to separate streams that often operate quite independently of each other. First, there is a 'stream of problems' that captures the attention of policy-makers in a government or an organization. Second, there is a policy community of specialists, which may include people inside or outside the organization, that concentrates on generating policy proposals. This is the 'stream of solutions' that float around in what is called 'primeval soup'. Some of these ideas and solutions are taken seriously, while others are not. The third ingredient, the 'political stream', is composed of elements such as public opinion, election results, changes in administration, ideological shifts, and interest group campaigns. Each of the actors and processes associated with these streams can function as either an impetus or a constraint to change. Although there may be some overlap and some connection between the streams, they are largely separate from each other, governed by different considerations and styles. For example, real problems with feasible solutions may not emerge on the policy agenda due to an absence of political support. And the lack of political support may reflect differences in ideology or a particular view of how the public might react to a particular proposal. For government, public opinion and the anticipated reactions of interest groups are particularly important during the pre-election period of their mandate.

While these streams usually operate independently, they do connect at times. This opens a 'policy window' that can lead to problem recognition, agenda setting, and the creation of new policies or programs. However, if these opportunities are missed (for example, if no action is taken or if the political mood shifts), then the policy window will close and the opportunity will be lost, at least for the time being.

A key stage in the process is problem recognition and definition. Recognition, according to Kingdon, generally occurs through three mechanisms. The first is a change in indicators such as unemployment rates, economic growth, interest rates, or the rate of children in care. A second mechanism is a 'focusing event' that directs attention and sometimes action in response to an issue. This may be a sudden and unpredictable event, such as the 1992 death of Matthew Vaudreuil in British Columbia, which helped to open a window for change in child welfare policy. The third mechanism is

## Box 3.3 The Value Criteria Model in Policy-Making

The development of West Region Child and Family Services in Manitoba illustrates how the value criteria model can be used to develop policies that shape an agency's overall orientation to practice and program development. Growing awareness of the child welfare system's colonizing effects in First Nations communities in the late 1970s and early 1980s led to the signing of a Master Agreement by Manitoba First Nations, the government of Manitoba, and the government of Canada in 1982. This Agreement paved the way for the transfer of administrative control of child welfare services to tribal council authorities in the province, and in 1985 West Region Child and Family Services, serving nine First Nations reserves, became a fully mandated child and family service agency. This agency paid special attention to assessing the impact of the conventional child welfare system on family and community life, an impact represented by the loss of hundreds of children from their families and communities, and by the presence of powerlessness within many of these families and communities. This led to the adoption of four key philosophical principles by the new agency that are used as guidelines for policy development. These principles, which may be expressed as value criteria, are Aboriginal control, cultural relevancy, community-based services, and a comprehensive team-oriented approach to service delivery. Thus, a service model has been adopted that relies on local staff working with local child and family service committees that have considerable authority. Specialized service teams have also been developed to provide support and back-up services to local staff. In addition, the agency adopts a broad approach to child and family services by undertaking initiatives in day care, family violence intervention, and community development.

Cultural relevancy shapes policy development through such things as an emphasis on hiring Aboriginal staff, providing culturally relevant staff training, and incorporating the wisdom of elders. Furthermore, the agency has played a leadership role in developing culturally appropriate foster homes, including the widespread use of extended family care. The agency is managed by a Board of Chiefs, but there are also extensive efforts to incorporate a broader level of community participation in policy development. For example, an Operational Planning Workshop is held every two years in which representatives from each community engage with agency staff in identifying new service needs and priorities. Today, very few children require care outside their community or their culture, and an external evaluation has demonstrated that the agency provides both a high standard of service quality and a supportive, sustaining work environment for its staff (Adapted from McKenzie, 1994).

normal feedback from the operation of programs; this includes the role of evaluation in influencing policy development.

Pal (1992, p. 135) elaborates on Kingdon's list of mechanisms leading to problem recognition by identifying criteria that can be used to determine when a problem becomes a *public* problem. In order to define something as a public problem, he suggests that the problem must affect a substantial proportion of the public, offend or affront widely held public views or mores, or be the direct result of previous public policies. Two examples may help to illustrate these processes. In the case of the Canada Pension Plan, actuarial information indicates that without substantial changes, the plan will be unable to meet future benefit payments for retiring Canadians. In addition, the crisis has been intensified by previous government policies that resulted in benefit payouts to beneficiaries that have been far in excess of the value of their contributions since inception. In this case, the problem affects a wide number of Canadians, and results, in part, from the failure of previous policies. This has led the federal government to adopt the controversial policy of substantial premium increases over the next several years. A second example concerns the Somalia crisis. To most Canadians, the actions of the military in Somalia have been an affront to our values and to our international reputation as 'peacekeepers'. These actions led to public recognition of serious problems within the Canadian military, even if the solutions adopted to date appear to stop short of addressing the fundamental problems of racism and cover-ups by senior levels of the military establishment.

It is often difficult to predict which issue will be defined as a public problem in that its recognition depends on a combination of objective data or stimuli and the subjective perception that change is required. Indeed, in some cases, subjective perceptions become more important than objective data. Youth violence in Winnipeg provides one such example. In recent years there has been growing concern about high levels of juvenile crime, particularly within the inner city. However, the actual rate of youth crime declined between 1994 and 1996. This has not prevented a growing perception among the public that youth crime is increasing, a perception fuelled by increasingly intense media attention on the operation of organized street gangs. In turn, this perception has led to heightened demands for a more primitive approach to the problem of youth crime.

Issues can remain on the policy agenda for some time, although the weighting of certain issues may vary at different times depending on how the three streams interact. Furthermore, items can fall off the policy agenda because they cannot be sustained or because the problem may appear to be 'solved'. For example, in the 1980s the need for a national day care strategy was widely recognized, and the federal Conservative government made a commitment at that time to launch such an initiative. However, the government retreated from this commitment and no major policy initiative occurred. Despite the lack of action, this issue received very little attention in the federal policy arena for most of the 1990s.

## **Table 3.1** Models of Policy-Making: A Summary

### A. *The Rational Model*[1]

1. Define the problem in objective terms and classify goals.
2. Develop a comprehensive list of alternatives to address the problem.
3. Project possible consequences and the probability of occurrence for each set of alternatives.
4. Examine data for each strategy in relation to goals and benefit-cost calculations.
5. Select a strategy to maximize goals and to achieve the best benefit-cost ratio.

### B. *Incrementalism*[2]

1. Calculate the marginal benefits of current choices for addressing the problem.
2. Initiate small choices toward a solution that would achieve marginal benefits.
3. Increase the emphasis on choices that produce positive results; reduce the emphasis on choices leading to negative results.
4. Policy emerges from a combination of choices that work.

### C. *Mixed Scanning*[3]

1. Define the problem and classify goals.
2. Conduct a comprehensive scan of alternatives.
3. Select alternatives for detailed analysis based on potential for goal achievement and feasibility.
4. Collect data and select the alternative best able to maximize goals and feasibility considerations.
5. Project incremental incorporation of policy choice.

### D. *The Value Criteria Model*[4]

1. Define the problem and identify policy alternatives available to deal with the problem.
2. Establish universal and selective criteria (values) for evaluating alternatives.
3. Gather data related to each alternative, and assess each alternative relative to benefit-cost considerations and value criteria.
4. Recommend an alternative that maximizes the value criteria, or offer a range of alternatives that maximize different criteria in different ways.

### E. *The Garbage Can Model*[5]

1. Three types of processes exist in agenda setting for policy-making. These are characterized as 'streams' of problems, solutions, and politics.
2. These streams exist somewhat independently of each other, but from time to time a window of opportunity opens when these three streams come together. A key stage is public recognition of a problem and three mechanisms can contribute to this stage. These are a change in economic or social indicators, an unpredictable event, or feedback from program operations.
3. Once a policy window opens, problems, solutions, and political opportunity are combined in a 'garbage can' and the outcome will depend on characteristics associated with the problems, alternatives, and participants included in the mix.
4. If the opportunity is missed or if appropriate action is taken, the policy window closes, and one must wait for the next opportunity. Issues can also sit on the policy agenda although they may be weighted differently at different times. In addition, items can fall off the policy agenda because they cannot be sustained or because the problem may appear to be solved.

Sources
[1]Adapted from Carley (1980, p. 11).
[2]Adapted from Lindblom (1959).
[3]Adapted from Etzioni (1976).
[4]Adapted from Dobelstein (1990, p. 71).
[5]Adapted from Kingdon (1995, pp. 86–8).

The garbage can model provides useful insight into the policy-making process as it unfolds, but it is less prescriptive about measures that can be undertaken to manage this process to realize intended goals. Despite this limitation, it does direct our intention to the importance of understanding and shaping the political processes that influence the various stages of policy formulation and adoption.

A summary of the policy-making steps in each of the general models is provided in Table 3.1, although we stress that these steps in policy development should be approached in an interactive manner over time rather than in a linear fashion. We have also presented each of these models as discrete approaches; in fact, in the real world of policy-making, a mix of more than one approach can often be identified.

## Assessing How Policy-Making Models Connect to Practice

To some extent, the major approaches to policy-making outlined in the previous section oversimplify the policy development process. In fact, policy-making is a process of trying to decide what to do in situations in which values and opinions often conflict and where the final choice is heavily shaped by differing ideologies. Given this reality, it follows that the product will reflect the values of those who are in pivotal positions, and, as noted earlier, these positions are occupied primarily by middle-aged and prosperous men. Their lives and experiences are vastly different from the service users and practitioners in the human services. Policy-making is about recognizing the legitimacy of a social problem, establishing the feasibility of a particular solution, and garnering support for the adoption of a preferred solution. Under these circumstances it is not surprising that those with power wield a disproportionate amount of influence over the policies that are eventually adopted.

It is essential to emphasize that regardless of the approach—whether rational and comprehensive or incremental—social policy is permeated by politics. In the last analysis, the major decisions are made by politicians and governments whose pre-eminent concern is to be re-elected. Thus, all important policies will be assessed through the political lens of votes: will this initiative help or hinder a party's chances of being re-elected? But government, and organizations for that matter, do not *always* follow the most politically expedient route. They are sometimes driven by causes that reflect a deeply held conviction or ideological commitment, and policy directions under these circumstances are not easily compromised. For example, the Saskatchewan NDP government, led by Tommy Douglas, withstood significant public pressure in 1961 when it adopted Canada's first medicare program. It is also apparent that Ontario's Conservative government under Mike Harris has enacted a series of social policy reforms that have resulted in widespread hardship to many. As demonstrated below, despite significant public protest the Ontario government shows little evidence of deviating from its relentless attack on welfare recipients, unions, and public services.

Directly through the 22 per cent cut in their monthly payments and indirectly through the cancellation of the Jobs Ontario program, the poorest of all Ontarians have been hit grossly disproportionately. Indeed, reduced spending on welfare recipients will account for a full one-third of the $1.4 billion in cuts that [finance minister] Eves announced. This move was necessary, the finance minister said, to head off a 'spending crisis'. In fact Eve's motive here was ideological rather than financial . . . . It is those on welfare who are paying for the ideological convictions of the Harris government (Gwyn, 1995, p. 4).

Politics and ideologies can have far-reaching effects in every policy area, including child welfare. At first glance one would think that ensuring the well-being of children should be divorced from politics and that the criteria for appointment to senior positions in child welfare should be based on competence and professional experience. Yet in recent years in British Columbia, four superintendents of child welfare have been fired not because of incompetence but because their ideologies were inconsistent with the government's or with the minister's. Indeed, the only superintendent not fired was a person who combined the roles of deputy minister and superintendent.

It is important to consider briefly how policy and practice might be connected within each policy-making model. At the outset we should acknowledge a difference in purpose between policy and practice that often creates a gap between the two that is difficult to bridge. Policies describe what should be done in general when confronted with a need or a problem, whereas practice is concerned about what should be done *in a specific situation*. Too often policies, when rigidly adopted, fail to consider the specific circumstances or needs of individuals or communities, which are, in fact, the primary concerns of practitioners. While this makes closing the gap between policy and practice difficult, it is self-evident that if policies are developed with more input from service users and practitioners, then policies will be more likely to be responsive to their needs and experiences. Moreover, if policies in the human services retain some elements of flexibility, practitioners will be able to adapt these to the particular needs of individuals, families, and communities.

Do any of the general policy-making models we have described ensure that the wisdom of practitioners and service users will be combined with that of policy-makers? The rational approach is primarily a top-down process that clearly assigns a primary role to policy analysts who are responsible for drafting new policies or legislation. It is an élite approach to planning in which pre-eminent roles are assigned to policy experts, and even when this approach incorporates far-reaching consultations, the eventual choices are made by a select few.

As the name suggests, incrementalism is a more informal process that may well facilitate partnerships between policy-makers and practitioners. Although a series of small steps can eventually lead to substantial changes, it is more likely that these steps will continue in a well-established direction, and will not significantly challenge accepted ways of doing things, whether in policy or practice. For example, in child welfare, incrementalism might result in the addition of new resources and programs, but it would not reframe the mission of child welfare in a fundamental fashion. Incrementalism is unlikely to lead to reforms in governance structures or to establish care-giving work as work requiring an equitable salary from the public purse. Indeed, incrementalism promotes and sustains a very comfortable environment: policy becomes routinized and practitioners become its caretakers. Although incrementalism allows for practitioner input, opportunities are not usually extended to service users, those who are the recipients of service. Like the rational approach, it is not seen here as the approach of choice. And since mixed scanning represents a combination of both the rational and the incremental approaches, it, too, represents a limited approach to connecting policy and practice.

The value criteria model is an adaptation of the rational model; however, it incorporates the explicit treatment of values. This is its most important strength, but its ability to serve as a useful tool in connecting policy and practice is highly dependent on what values are selected for consideration and on how the process of value analysis is conducted. For example, if the value criteria used in policy selection incorporate the concerns of practitioners and service users, the potential for meaningful connections between policy and practice is enhanced. However, if values reflect the concerns of centralized policy-makers who remain distant from the day-to-day concerns of front-line staff and service users, this model will also fail to integrate these two domains.

The garbage can model of policy-making incorporates political processes as a consideration in policy adoption. Also, a role for policy communities that may lie outside the decision-making structures is recognized in that they advocate for recognition of a specific issue as a public problem and contribute to the stream of solutions by recommending particular policies. While practitioners and service users may be involved in these policy communities their involvement is often quite limited. One of the reasons is that such policy communities must usually sustain their efforts over a relatively long time even to obtain relatively modest gains; thus, it is often difficult to attract and retain the involvement of practitioners or service users.

Each of these approaches may be adapted to be more inclusive in ways that increase the potential of connecting policy and practice; however, none insist on inclusiveness. The value criteria model comes closest to realizing this potential in that it allows for the specification of value criteria that can include consultation and/or decision-making input from practitioners and service users. Clearly, this policy-making model must adopt the central principle of inclusiveness if it is to succeed in connecting policy and practice concerns. But in order to achieve this principle, policy-making must be transformed from a process in which decisions are made in secret at the highest level of the organization, and then packaged within this arena for marketing to an apparently resistant and largely uninformed group of practitioners and service users. As indicated by the example in Box 3.4, policy-makers seem to demonstrate an all-too-frequent pattern of failing to include those who will not be affected by the adoption of new policies.

### Box 3.4 Policy-Making and the Failure to Consult with Those Affected

In March, 1997 a high-level policy forum on gang crime was convened in Winnipeg to discuss the growing problem of inner-city youth gangs dominated by Aboriginal young people. While two federal cabinet ministers, provincial cabinet ministers, policy officials, the mayor of Winnipeg, and other leaders met at an inner-city location, dozens of Aboriginal people were barred from entry. Only after arguing with security staff for some time were a small group of representatives from the Native Youth Movement allowed in, and then only on the condition that they keep quiet. After about an hour, at the moderator's invitation, two representatives delivered an impassioned presentation to community leaders who responded with an enthusiastic ovation at the end of the presentation. One of the presenters argued that the focus must be to rebuild the social structure and the family unit within the Aboriginal community to resemble the structures that existed before colonization. The other Aboriginal young person allowed to speak urged participants to bring young people to the table. (Adapted from Nairne, 1997.)

---

It must also be acknowledged that the controversy concerning the policy process also occurs within the practice arena itself. As noted above, the rational approach is based on systems theory and the scientific method, while other approaches depart from these traditions to varying degrees. The differences in the various approaches are to a large extent mirrored by the debate surrounding the use of research and the scientific method in social work practice. The opposing positions in the debate are espoused by two eminent social work educators. The position that social work practice should be based on empirical research is expressed by Edward Mullen in relation to the problem of AIDS. He argues that:

> [the] scientific method requires that the practitioner determine what has already been found out through prior study to be effective ways for helping people deal with impending depression and what is known about these methods with people with AIDS. Scientific criteria also require that social workers systematically evaluate their own attempts to help people with AIDS cope with impending depression. (Mullen, 1992, p. 111)

The opposing position is expressed by Howard Goldstein, who believes that the scientific method is too rigid and too confining as a template for social work practice:

> Professor Mullen perpetuates the seductive myth of the scientific method and its promises of professional status and respectability. It defines social work as a technology that can discover the causes of human suffering and despair, devise pre-

cise interventions and predict outcomes. Our heritage and practice prove that social work is not a technology, but rather a humanistic endeavour in which artistry, creativity, intuitiveness and interpersonal talents are hallmarks of our professional competencies. (Goldstein, 1992, p. 113)

It is not difficult to argue with some of the ideas and beliefs associated with both of these positions. One solution is to try to identify the best in both positions. However, in the field of social policy we are inclined to agree with Rittel and Webber (1973, p. 158), who state:

As distinguished from problems in the natural sciences which are definable and separable and may have solutions that are findable, the problems of governmental planning—and especially those of social or policy planning—are ill defined: and they rely on elusive political judgment for resolution. (Not 'solution'. Social problems are never solved. At best they are only re-solved—over and over again.)

The next chapter extends the discussion of policy-making by introducing the stages of the policy-making process. These stages provide a beginning framework for some of the analytical tasks that must be undertaken in policy development.

# 4
## Stages and Structures in the Policy-Making Process

## The Stages of the Policy-Making Process

While the rational model insists that the policy-making process can and should be divided into discrete stages with attendant structures and actors, incrementalism argues that such discreteness is undesirable since the stages slip and slide into one another in a random fashion. Nevertheless, in order to understand the process of policy-making it is helpful to identify the stages, and then to acknowledge that a good deal of overlap does occur. The five stages, outlined in Figure 4.1, are similar to the stages that might be used in assessment and intervention in a practice context. We discuss each stage in turn and emphasize the similarities between policy-making and practice processes.

**Figure 4.1** Corresponding Stages of Policy and Practice Processes

| Policy-Making | Practice |
|---|---|
| Initiation | Problem Identification |
| Formulation | Developing action plans |
| Execution | Deciding on the plan |
| Implementation | Implementation |
| Evaluation | Evaluation |

### The Initiation Stage

In both policy-making and practice, action or change begins at a discernible point. In practice, the beginning point might take the form of a request by a client for assistance, a referral from another agency, or a complaint by a neighbour or fellow professional. In policy-making the beginning point might emanate from a social movement pushing for change, from staff in a ministry who have become convinced of the inadequacy of existing policy, or from a government that in its role as official Opposition or because of its political constituency has become committed to making changes.

In all the possible scenarios, a 'convergence of interest' (Sower et al., 1957) or a crisis of some magnitude must occur before action will be initiated. As conceptualized by Sower et al., a convergence of interest includes the notion of an idea whose time has come: the perception that something simply has to be done about condition x. In the garbage can model of policy development a convergence of interest is defined as a 'window of opportunity' that occurs when the political stream, the stream of problems, and the stream of solutions come together. A convergence of interest is often influenced by the characteristics of the person or organization pushing for change; these characteristics include authority, legitimacy, and commitment. Thus, an agency director may have the authority to propose a change but may lack the confidence of the agency's staff. A change proposed by such a director may be initiated but it will encounter problems during the change process. Conversely, a long-standing staff member who is highly regarded by colleagues may lack authority but may nevertheless possess a high degree of legitimacy. Both of these people will need to back their proposal with energy and commitment; indeed, causes backed by a dedicated champion may well succeed despite the absence of other factors usually considered essential in bringing about change.

The probability is that a convergence of interest is expanded here to include the availability of resources, the complexity of the change, the context or environment, and timing. Thus, a relatively simple change proposed by and backed by the commitment and resources of a minister of social services or a minister of health in a sympathetic environment will in all likelihood be initiated. However, the scenario will shift if the minister's proposal involves a complex issue about which there is wide and vehement disagreement. As we noted earlier, controversial issues will likely be referred to some type of study group. The prospects of a successful launch are remote if the proposal for change emanates from a back-bencher of a party in opposition or from a professional organization lacking close connections with the minister and the party in power.

The explanatory power of the concept of convergence of interest takes a different form in the event of a crisis such as the death of a child. Crises can provoke new unanticipated actions, especially if they can be used to reinforce the agendas of those in positions of power and if resources are available. Thus, the 1992 death of Matthew Vaudreuil in British Columbia was interpreted by the minister and senior staff in charge of child welfare as justification to inquire into the internal working conditions of the department and the practices of the front-line staff. In this example, Judge Gove was appointed to conduct a far-reaching investigation of child welfare practices in the province, and his recommendations led to major organizational and service delivery changes in this field.

In practice, initiation often begins with a complaint or a referral that is accepted by the agency. Again, the likelihood of acceptance is much greater if the request comes from a respectable and well-known source. When faced with referrals from unknown or poorly regarded sources and by requests from clients who have earned a reputation for being difficult, rude, or antagonistic, staff might delay responses or ignore the request. Again, a crisis often spurs a prompt response regardless of the source of the referral or the reputation of the client.

The most perplexing part of the initiation stage revolves around defining the problem to be addressed. Social problems are notoriously difficult to pin down and yet the definition sets the stage for the rest of the policy-making process. Indeed, the very term 'definition' is problematic since it connotes precision and explicitness. We prefer the term 'framing', which outlines the general parameters of the issue being addressed.

Framing provides a sense of direction. It sets out preferences and prescribes limits based on ideologies and experiences, but refrains from the explicitness expected of a definition. Although Rittel and Webber use 'definition' rather than 'framing', the essence of the latter notion is captured by their description of social problems as 'wicked problems'.

Wicked problems have a number of distinguishing properties, for example:

a)  there is no definitive formulation of a wicked problem;
b)  wicked problems have no stopping rule: they are resolved over and over again;
c)  solutions to wicked problems are not true-false but good or bad—depending on one's values and experience;
d)  every solution to a wicked problem is a 'one shot operation'; because there is no opportunity to learn by trial and error every attempt counts significantly;
e)  every wicked problem is essentially unique; and
f)  every wicked problem is a symptom of another problem (Rittel and Webber, 1973, pp. 167–8).

In our view, framing the problem is the most significant aspect of the initiation stage. Thus, if the problem of poverty is framed as the unwillingness of citizens to work, then the solution would be to force people to work or to provide incentives so that more individuals will find and keep employment. Similarly, if the problem is framed simply as the lack of employment opportunities, then attention would focus on job creation programs. However, if poverty is defined as the consequence of a number of faulty and interlocking public policies, including educational preparation, the appropriate structure and the failure to establish a progressive tax system, then the task becomes one of examining the very concept of work, who receives compensation, and whether there are sufficient opportunities for employment. Framing the problem in this way implies the need for more comprehensive and radical changes.

Practitioners face similar dilemmas in the problem identification phase of practice. Should a single-parent mother be viewed as a disadvantaged and distressed person with limited resources doing her best to manage under difficult circumstances? If so, then the appropriate response would be to assist her by increasing her resources and reducing her stress. Conversely, the identification of the same person as requiring training in parenting and budgeting skills will result in referrals to suitable training programs.

An illuminating example of framing in practice relates to the project touched on in Chapter 1 (see Box 4.1).

### Box 4.1 Framing the Problem in the Empowering Women Project

The Empowering Women Project in British Columbia brought together child welfare workers and their clients and asked them to find ways to meet the needs of clients and to change child welfare practice. The first step was to identify a number of clients interested in the project, to convene a group meeting, and to develop action plans. The co-ordinator of the project was a former child protection worker. In her previous role her relationship with service users typically began with an investigation of a complaint of neglect or abuse. She acknowledged that her assessments of possible neglect or abuse, were, like those of her colleagues, based on pinpointing problems and deficits: is there evidence of abuse and/or neglect? Are there indications of a poor marital relationship? Are the parents immature? Is the available income adequate? Is the housing satisfactory?

The co-ordinator of the project now works with service users in a completely different way because her assessments are framed by interactions with a group of motivated women eager to address issues and identify solutions. This frame focuses on strengths: for example, one woman was a carpenter, another was a day-care worker, and a third was an experienced secretary. From the perspective of the people who use services, the opportunity to identify problems, to discuss solutions, and to work with the co-ordinator as a source of assistance rather than as an investigator also altered the women's framing experience substantially. These women felt validated and motivated to take action in a way that had not occurred to them in the past.

The example in Box 4.1 illustrates the power of framing in setting the course of the policy-making and practice processes. In fact, the framing of wicked problems is set largely by ideologies. We argue that most of those who have wielded influence in framing and developing social policies in the 90s have been driven by ideologies that are conservative and that view government intervention as a last resort. These frames have set the context for practice and a deep and continuing faultline has been created by the gap between the needs of service users and the policies ostensibly designed to serve them. As a result, practitioners are forced to divert energy into either ignoring the gap or finding ways of straddling it.

The actors in the initiation stage of policy-making vary from citizens or professionals in social movements, to staff of government departments, to politicians. When an individual has the power to insist that change should begin, as in the case of a minister of social services who wishes to establish an inquiry into the death of a child, the policy-making process can be set in motion fairly easily. Others, such as staff in direct service positions or in low-level administrative jobs, lack the authority to initiate such actions directly. Such individuals must not only be seen as legitimate and knowledgeable but also must be able to establish links with policy-makers in order to initiate policy change.

However, the initiation of change can result from persistent campaigns by those affected either by the absence of a policy or by an inadequate policy. Examples include the efforts of the feminist movement to establish transition houses for battered women and to change hiring practices in the work force; and the struggle of First Nations people to settle land claims and to achieve self-government. In Chapter 8 the efforts of a policy community of service users and citizens to change guardianship legislation in British Columbia are described in some detail.

Finally, we should note that when initiation involves issues that are controversial or have significant budgetary implications, the decision to proceed will be made by the governing body: the premier and the Cabinet in the provincial and federal government, the council in a municipal government, and the board of directors in voluntary agencies.

### The Formulation Stage
The second stage of the policy-making process—formulation—involves developing and analysing alternatives. At this stage the methods of policy analysis come into play; the next chapter presents a detailed discussion of this topic. Even though the major thrust or direction for change may have been set by the manner in which the problem has been framed, a number of different responses will still need to be considered. Thus, in formulating a 'get tough' response to delinquency, policy-makers may want to consider whether expanding police forces is preferable to an increase in the number of juvenile detention facilities, and, within the latter option, whether wilderness camps are preferred to other forms of imprisonment.

Formulation is the stage in which techniques from the rational approach become most useful. Formulating alternatives may begin in brainstorming sessions in which no suggestion, however improbable, is rejected. Once all possible alternatives have been identified, they are analysed on the basis of previously accepted criteria. Such criteria might include the anticipated cost, the feasibility of implementation, the benefits to the political party in power, and possible outcomes for beneficiaries. As will be obvious from this beginning list, criteria are not of the same order or importance. Do gains to the party outweigh costs? Do benefits to clients take precedence over ease of implementation?

Royal commissions and task forces are favourite vehicles for dealing with complex issues at the formulation stage. These structures have a number of advantages to those in power: they give the appearance of action while buying time before a decision is required, and they assure everyone that the problem is being studied in depth by experts. But royal commissions can produce surprises and none was more surprising than the outcomes of the Royal

Commission on Taxation (McQuaig, 1987). This commission was established by a Conservative government and the members appointed to the Commission were, in terms of background and experience, equally conservative in their views of fiscal policy. The government was confident that, after due course and proper study, the commission would conclude that the existing tax structure was basically sound and that only minor changes were warranted. However, the assignment required that commission members immerse themselves in every aspect of taxation, including country-by-country comparisons, the pros and cons of capital gains and inheritance taxes, deferred arrangements for corporations, and loopholes. This examination led some members, including the influential chair, Kenneth Carter, to fundamentally alter their views and to recommend sweeping changes (McQuaig, 1987).

An integral part of royal commissions and task forces is inviting the public to attend hearings and to submit briefs and these invitations are often taken up by a large number of individuals and groups. For example, the Community Panel that reviewed child welfare in British Columbia prior to the formulation of the *Child, Family and Community Service Act* (1994) 'heard 550 presentations in more than 23 communities and received over 600 written briefs from individuals and groups' (Durie and Armitage, 1996, p. 19). In such circumstances a vast amount of information is gathered, organized, and classified according to the themes that have emerged; analysed to permit the identification of findings and recommendations; and, finally, translated into policy and/or legislation by policy analysts or legislative drafters.

While governments that follow this approach can claim that they consulted the public prior to making a choice among competing options, there is nevertheless no real accountability in representing the views of the public fairly. Thus, governments may select those views that are more consistent with their particular perspective. The consultation process is open to even more criticism when, as in the case of the 1994–5 review of Canada's social security system,[1] the nature of the inquiry was carefully orchestrated by policy-makers, including the selection of who was to be allowed to present briefs. In this example, the distillation of public input begins with controlling who can provide this input.

One useful way of analysing the extent of the influence of citizens in the policy-making process is provided by a framework called 'a ladder of citizen participation' (Arnstein, 1969). The ladder has eight rungs (see Figure 4.2). The top three rungs—citizen control, delegated power, and partnerships—represent differing degrees of citizen power. The next three, which include placation, consultation, and informing, symbolize degrees of tokenism. Consultation, the middle rung of this group, allows 'the have-nots to hear and have a voice, but . . . they lack the power to ensure that their views will be heeded by the powerful' (Arnstein, 1969, p. 217). The two bottom rungs refer to processes that do not enable participation; then include therapy and manipulation. We refer again to this useful conceptualization in the discussion of community governance in Chapter 9.

**Figure 4.2** A Ladder of Citizen Participation

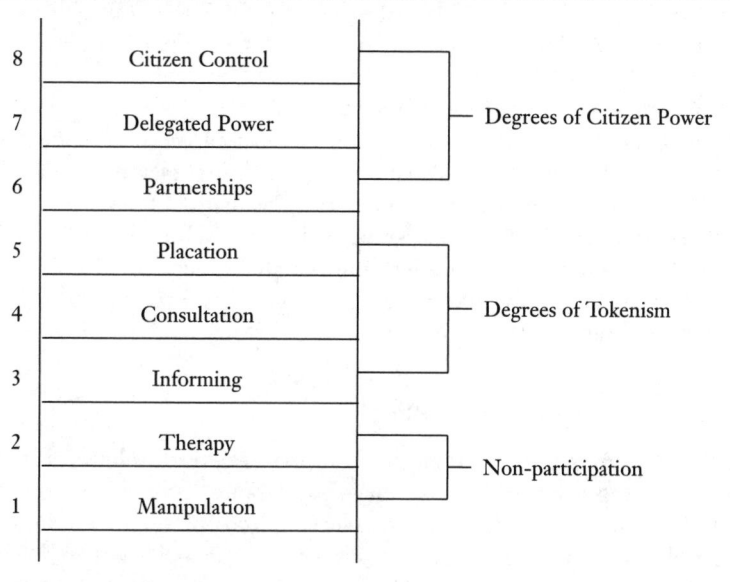

Source: Reproduced from Arnstein, 1969, p. 217.

Like their policy counterparts, professionals in direct practice must develop an action plan, and tasks undertaken in completing an assessment provide the basis for such a plan. As in policy formulation, this phase may be extensive and elaborate, involving a number of people and generating several optional strategies. In some cases the phase may be brief and yield only one plan. The latter is likely to occur when the medical model holds sway and a plan is developed by the practitioner or by an external expert. On the other hand, if a partnership approach exists, action plans will be developed jointly by the practitioner and the service user, perhaps with the input of experts. In these circumstances, it is more likely that a wider range of options will be considered.

**The Execution Stage**
At the execution stage, choices are reviewed and a decision is made. In federal and provincial policy matters, recommendations involving major changes and/or a substantial increase in resources will be reviewed by analysts within the Treasury Board before being forwarded to the premier and the Cabinet for decision. When the policy takes the form of new legislation or changes to existing Acts, the Cabinet will review and approve these plans prior to sending the Act to the legislature for debate and final decision.

In a voluntary agency the board of directors will decide whether to proceed with the plans. Prior to doing so, it may refer recommendations made by committees comprising board and staff members to outside consultants or to standing committees of finance and personnel.

The execution stage in practice rests essentially with the practitioner and the service user. This is most often referred to as the contracting stage, in which goals, objectives, tasks, and activities for ongoing work are outlined.

### Implementation and Evaluation Stages
Implementation and evaluation are the two final phases of the policy process, and these focus on the delivery and evaluation of services and programs resulting from policy development. The evaluation phase is discussed in more detail in the next chapter, since evaluation techniques and activities are closely connected to the topic of policy analysis. Because of the importance of the implementation phase in connecting policy-making and practice, we devote Chapter 6 to this topic.

## Structures in Policy-Making

All organizations create formal mechanisms—referred to here as *structures*—for developing policy. Structures vary considerably depending on the size, age, and complexity of the organization. The simplest structures are found in small, relatively new voluntary organizations. In such agencies either the board of directors or a subcommittee of the board assumes responsibility for developing policy. When the subcommittee structure is selected, and depending on the commitment of the agency to the principle of inclusiveness, a cross-section of staff, board members, and the individuals being served may be involved in the work of the subcommittee. Such 'vertical slices' represent a determined effort to ensure the participation of all affected by the agency and its services.

While the structure may be simple, the debates that occur in the process of developing policy are often lengthy and contentious. One of the authors recalls discussions in a John Howard Society when the agency developed a position on accepting financial assistance from the federal and provincial governments. Given the often precarious financial situation of the agency, some board members argued strongly in favour of accepting any and all offers of assistance. Others responded by noting that funding from governments would limit the agency's ability to criticize the services provided by the state. On this particular occasion the Board adopted a policy against accepting financial assistance from government.

The features of simplicity and inclusiveness that characterize policy-making structures in voluntary agencies are rarely found in governments, particularly those at the provincial and federal levels. Policy-making structures in the public sector are numerous, complex, and elaborate. While the names, numbers, and responsibilities of structures differ from province to province and are constantly being reorganized in attempts to improve efficiency, the following describes the typical array of structures established by governments.

First, it is important to note that policy-making in government occurs on three levels: matters internal to the ministry; orders-in-council that require the assent of the Cabinet; and changes to legislation that need the approval of the legislature. The complexity of the structures increases with each level of approval. While temporary and time-limited, royal commissions, judicial inquiries, and task forces also represent important policy-making structures, and we discuss these bodies and their roles in policy-making elsewhere in the book.

In most instances the initial work on new or revised policy proposals is handled by a program division within ministries. Thus, an income assistance division will take responsibility for beginning the process of making changes to the eligibility requirements for social assistance. After being drafted and approved by the program division and its director, proposals are forwarded to the ministry's policy and planning branch.

Policy and planning branches or units constitute one of the two formal policy-making structures within ministries, the second being the ministry's Executive Committee or Council responsible for making final decisions on all ministry matters. Branches are responsible for preparing analyses of existing policies; for reviewing proposals emanating from outside the ministry that have an impact on the ministry; and for the final drafting of proposals from program divisions. Policy and planning branches ensure that all proposals follow a common format; that all proposals have carefully considered the financial implications and have been reviewed through one or more lenses (e.g., gender, health, environment); and that appropriate stakeholders have been consulted. When the branch is satisfied that a proposal meets all the criteria, the proposal is sent to the Executive Council. Typically this structure consists of the deputy minister and the assistant deputies responsible for the various program divisions, finance, and communication. During the process of deliberation the deputy consults on a regular basis with the minister and with his/her aides to ensure that they are in agreement and can contribute information based on their knowledge and perspectives.

The second level of policy-making refers to changes in the regulations that surround and interpret legislation. Such changes, called orders-in-council, require approval from Cabinet. Prior to being considered by Cabinet, these proposals are reviewed by a Cabinet committee typically called the Priorities and Planning Committee. When there are financial implications, proposals are reviewed by the Treasury Board chaired by the minister of finance and, at the federal level, by the president of the Treasury Board. In recent, fiscally-conscious times, Treasury Boards have assumed an ever-increasing role in the policy-making process at all levels of government. Indeed, the influence of Treasury Boards and of finance ministries has done much to bring about the 'fiscalization of social policy' (Rice and Prince, 1993). Again, Cabinet submissions must conform to a specific format that requires appropriate consultation and a review by the Treasury Board, and that specifies the pros and cons of the proposal from both a service and a political perspective. Thus, the proposal must specify the benefits to recipients and the political mileage to be gained. If the two goals conflict, key players in Cabinet and in the Office of the Premier attempt to bring about a resolution. If negotiations fail, the final decisions are often decided in favour of political criteria.

The third level comes into play when legislative changes are proposed. Such changes are introduced into the Legislative Assembly by the responsible minister. New legislation is given first, second, and final reading, which allows time for extensive and often heated debates. All new legislation requires prior approval from the Treasury Board, from Cabinet, and from the Premier's Office. In recent times, Premier's Offices have become the most powerful structures in the government. Examples abound: Ralph Klein in Alberta, Mike Harris in Ontario, Lucien Bouchard in Quebec, Frank McKenna in New Brunswick, and Glen Clark in British Columbia. Indeed, the deputy minister of the Premier's Office is often cited as the third most powerful individual in government, after the premier and the finance minister.

As complex as the policy-making structures of provincial governments are, they pale by comparison with those of the federal government. Since the days of Prime Minister Pierre Trudeau (1968–79, 1980–4), prime ministers have sought to balance the policy-making initiatives of ministries with their own analytic capacities. While the two principal policy-making structures—the Privy Council Office (PCO) and the Prime Minister's Office (PMO)—have existed since the early days of the federal government, they have received increased resources and responsibilities in recent years. In addition, the federal government has a planning and priorities committee of Cabinet, with responsibilities roughly equivalent to the provincial Cabinet committees on planning and priorities. Like the Premier's Office, the Prime Minister's Office collects and coordinates information about political matters.

Other influential structures at the federal level include the Ministry of Finance, the Treasury Board, the Ministry of Intergovernmental Affairs, and the Senate. With the exception of the Senate, these structures have become so powerful that Parliament often plays a primarily ceremonial role in the policy-making process. Doern and Phidd make this point in their summary of the policy-making process:

> There is, of course, little dispute that the executive branch of Cabinet-parliamentary government is the fulcrum of policy-making. This applies to the role of the prime minister and other Cabinet ministers, but also to the role of the senior bureaucracy and the central agency apparatus that supports the Cabinet. (Doern and Phidd, 1992, p. 27)

The significant part played by these centralized policy-making structures means that decisions are often made far from and are only distantly connected to the needs and concerns of first-line practitioners and those who receive services. Given this context, processes involving shared decision-making, an increased role for policy communities, and community governance, as discussed in Chapters 7 through 9, represent a significant departure from traditional approaches to policy-making.

## 5

### Analysing and Evaluating Social Policies

This chapter has three objectives. The first is to identify the process of social policy analysis as it applies to policy-making; the connections between policy analysis and evaluation are explored in relation to this objective. The second objective is to identify a generic model that may be useful in analysing social policies. Finally, we summarize general approaches to policy evaluation, particularly in circumstances where the results from other programs or pilot projects are being considered in developing new policies.

#### Policy Analysis in the Human Services

Policy analysis involves the identification and assessment of preferred alternatives to complex policy problems or issues. While it may include the assessment of a policy that has already been implemented, this type of assessment is more properly referred to as policy evaluation. As noted in Chapter 4, policy analysis involves activities carried out during the formulation stage in the policy-making process, and it is primarily concerned with predicting the future consequences of different policy options. This requires a focus on both technical data and the political aspects of decision-making. Because policy analysis makes an effort to predict the anticipated outcomes of policy alternatives, it often considers evaluation studies conducted on similar policies that have been implemented elsewhere. Alternatively, a new policy may be implemented as a pilot project with an attached evaluation component designed to estimate the consequences of widespread adoption of that particular policy choice. Policy analysis and policy research or evaluation are closely connected, although we need to point out an important distinction between the two sets of activities. Whereas policy analysis examines a particular social problem and alternative ways to solve that problem, social policy evaluation attempts to measure the precise effects of a particular policy response that is already in place. Thus, policy evaluation is similar to program evaluation in attempting to assess the effects of existing social programs.

In direct practice within the social services, the assessment phase follows problem identification and the development of a beginning contract for work. For example, a referral of possible abuse in child welfare may involve a preliminary investigation regarding the allegation. If there is sufficient cause for further involvement, this will include a more detailed assessment of whether abuse has occurred, the nature of the incident, whether there were previous incidents of abuse, and the future risk to the child. As well, a worker will consider what treatment options are required to address trauma arising from the abuse, and perform some kind of risk assessment. Is the child at future risk if left at home? Would a support worker in the home minimize risk and enable the child to remain at home? Should the child be placed in a foster home? If the offender is in the home, should the offender be removed? Predicting the future consequences of these options is a part of the assessment phase in direct practice, and it leads to the development of an action plan.

A similar process is involved in policy analysis, although here the intent is to assess the consequences flowing from policy choices affecting large numbers of service users or the public. For example, increased concern about the effects of sexual abuse on school-aged children in a community may encourage a local school board, in co-operation with public health and child welfare agencies, to consider a range of early intervention programs as one possible response. A number of questions may need to be answered in completing the analysis stage pertaining to this policy issue. Is there enough evidence of need to justify a program? How might parents respond? What kinds of programs exist and how effective are they? Is it necessary to adapt a program to meet the specific needs of the community in question? What would it cost to deliver such a program? Let us suppose that the answers to these questions lead to the decision to recommend that the local school board introduce an educational awareness program designed to prevent child abuse. This step brings us to the culmination of the formulation stage in the policy-making process just as the recommendation of what to do with an abused child moves the assessment tasks in direct practice towards the formulation of an action plan.

The policy example described above also illustrates the key work phases in policy analysis. These involve completing a detailed analysis of the problem or need, including available resources and options; estimating the future impact of various policy alternatives; and identifying and applying criteria for selecting the preferred alternative.

The problem analysis phase involves careful consideration of both objective and subjective aspects of the problem. For example, we need to be concerned with how many people are affected by the issue as well as with how they feel about and react to the issue.

The problem analysis phase may also involve conducting a needs assessment. While many methods may be used, including public hearings and social indicator data, such as poverty rates, needs studies often involve evaluation research methods. Such studies may involve developing a socioeconomic profile of the community, documenting those needs that pertain specifically to the policy or intervention being considered, and identifying factors likely to affect services. Needs studies are very important in policy analysis because a new policy initiative is seldom undertaken without demonstrable evidence of need. For example, the development of needle exchange programs in Canadian cities was based on evidence linking the multiple use of needles to the spread of HIV.

While needs assessment studies are important in policy-making, we argue that they reflect a deficit-oriented approach to analysis unless they are combined with an assessment of strengths and capacities. Here again, a parallel between policy and practice can be drawn. In the human services, there is a growing awareness of the need to build on strengths at the individual, family, and community level in order to promote change, and this process begins with an identification of existing strengths and resources as an important aspect of the assessment stage (see Saleebey, 1997). McKnight and Kretzmann (1992) apply a similar approach to policy-making at the community level in suggesting that needs-oriented assessments give us only half the picture. What is required to complete the picture is an identification of strengths and resources—a process described as 'mapping community capacity'.

Using the community as an example, three types or levels of strengths and assets must to be considered. First, there are the assets and strengths of individuals and organizations within the community that are largely subject to community control. Next are the assets located within the community that are largely controlled by outsiders. These assets may include both private and public institutions such as hospitals, schools, and social service agencies. Finally, there are potential building blocks that include those resources originating outside the neighbourhood that are controlled by outsiders. These may include actual or potential social transfer payments and capital improvement expenditures. With this kind of information, a policy analyst is in a better position to address existing needs by building both on identified strengths and on potential resources. While the principle of assessing strengths and resources is perhaps easier to apply in the case of a geographic community, it can also be applied to groups linked through affiliation or interest. In order to make a more helpful contribution to the policy-making process, conventional approaches to needs assessment must be modified to incorporate procedures that develop an inventory of resources and capacities.

Although value issues are involved throughout the policy analysis process, values become explicit when criteria are applied to decision-making. Sometimes these values are specified by decision-makers as parameters to guide the preferred policy choice; in other cases these criteria may be shaped by the analyst's own perspective. More often than not the decision-making process involved in recommending a preferred policy choice will involve some combination of the two.

The tasks in policy analysis are also affected by the scope of the problem or issue being considered. For example, estimating the policy effects resulting from changes to Unemployment Insurance (now called Employment Insurance) is a more complex undertaking than an analysis of programming options for adolescent sex offenders in a particular community. Nevertheless, the general process is similar.

One framework to help guide this process is outlined by Majchrzak (1984). She suggests that the first step is to understand the sociopolitical environment. In the case of a major government policy initiative, this involves activities such as identifying the problem and key policy issues, analysing the legislative history of these policy issues, obtaining organizational charts of decision-making bodies, drawing a model of the policy-making process, and interviewing stakeholders. If an analyst is conducting a policy study of treatment alternatives for adolescent sex offenders, one option may be a group home located in a particular community. Here, understanding the sociopolitical environment may involve gathering information on zoning issues and processes, identifying local community leadership, and specifying potential community responses to such an initiative.

The second step suggested by Majchrzak is the technical analysis of options, and this may involve methods such as a literature review, field experiments, qualitative methods, case studies, and cost-utility analysis. Tentative policy recommendations emerge from the technical analysis stage, and in a research study, these would signify the end of the process. However, the importance of assessing feasibility and implementation issues in policy analysis suggests that recommendations should be weighed with these considerations in mind. This might involve a review of potential costs and available resources, as well as an assessment of the anticipated responses by stakeholders. While feasibility issues alone or the probability of the adoption of the recommendations should not dictate the results of a policy study, this information may lead to modifications in the recommendations that will enhance the likelihood of adoption without jeopardizing the major purpose of the preferred policy option.

The 'doing' part of policy analysis involves the exercise of skills that have been associated with the field of policy-practice (Janssen, 1994). These include analytical, political, interactional, and value-clarifying skills. In the human services these skills must be exercised within a general model or method that connects essential elements of the macro-environment with issues closely related to the delivery of services. This connection to what are often referred to as 'issues on the ground' is essential if policies are to matter to practitioners. And, just like the assessment stage in direct practice, any approach to policy analysis should include the perspective of service users as well as practitioners.

## Using a Special Lens for Policy Analysis

Approaches to policy analysis can be distinguished by the relative emphasis placed on content or process issues. A content approach stresses the actual ingredients of a policy, that is, the substance of the policy, its goals and value preferences, and the types of benefits it provides (see Chambers, 1986). The actual contents of policies are important because these are related to actual or anticipated consequences. However, content approaches pay limited attention to how policies emerge and why they are developed in a particular fashion. For example, content approaches pay little attention to the political processes that shape policy-making and the trade-offs and compromises that may characterize the policy development stage. As noted in Chapter 3, this is one of the appealing attributes of the garbage can model of policy-making. A pure content approach to policy analysis also tends to reinforce an élitist approach to policy analysis in that the policy expert, as armchair critic, gathers data on the policy issue, subjects these data to critical scrutiny, and draws conclusions about the impact of the policy.

Without minimizing the importance of analyses of policy content, often developed to stimulate debate and dialogue about the policy, we argue that process considerations must also be included as components in a preferred model for policy analysis. A process approach to policy analysis pays more attention to who influences the development of policies, how action is generated, and who makes decisions (Flynn, 1992). There are two important advantages to including such considerations in policy analysis. First, while these considerations do not guarantee an increased role for practitioners and service users, they focus attention on characteristics that encourage these questions to be raised. Policy analysis and policy-making from a process perspective are also understood as an ongoing set of activities that involves creating and adapting policies and programs. Thus, it is consistent with an approach that encourages ongoing inclusiveness and connections between practice and policy. Second, process questions such as who influences policy development and how policy provisions are implemented enable the use of policy analysis to influence the changes to particular policies or programs. Policy-making, as outlined here then, is not a one-shot exercise but a continuing process of policy evolution. Indeed, new policies, with some exceptions, are most often old policies that have been changed or adapted to a different policy environment or set of circumstances.

Process considerations place an emphasis on policy analysis as an exercise in information-sharing as well as information-gathering; in addition, the process may include negotiation and partisan-based advocacy. At the end of the day, any analysis of policies must be designed to make a contribution to policy-making or policy change. If policy analysis is not undertaken with this goal in mind it will remain aloof from practice and disconnected from the change process.

One approach that integrates content and process concerns is the identification of a special lens or focus, often framed as a series of questions, to assess the particular impact of a policy on special populations. An example of this approach is the family impact model (Spakes, 1984). In this particular approach, policies are assessed for their impact on the membership function in families, the economic function, and the socialization/nurturance function. A series of questions is identified to guide such an assessment, for example:

a) Does the policy strengthen or erode the stability of the family?
b) Does the policy provide adequate support to different types of families?

This approach to the identification of particular impacts has broader relevance in focusing policy attention on traditionally neglected aspects of the policy-making process. For example, health and social service policy questions that focus on effects related to women, minority groups, and front-line service providers can be routinely incorporated as components of policy analysis if this approach is adapted to reflect such considerations. Two examples of such frameworks follow.

An Aboriginal framework for social work practice has been proposed by Morrissette, McKenzie, and Morrissette (1993); it includes four key principles. These are: (a) recognition of a distinct Aboriginal worldview; (b) recognition of the impact of colonialism; (c) recognition of cultural knowledge and traditions as an active component of sustaining Aboriginal identity and collective consciousness; and (d) empowerment as sustained through Aboriginal participation and control of essential components of the model. While these principles reflect general guidelines for the development of culturally appropriate approaches to social work practice, they also identify principles relevant to the development of a cultural lens for policy analysis.

A more elaborate framework for assessing the impact of a policy on women's equality has been developed by the British Columbia Ministry of Women's Equality (1994). This framework identifies two general questions for determining the gender implications of any policy:

a) Does the policy discriminate against women in its outcomes?
b) Does it support full participation and equality for women?

The gender-lens framework proposed in these guidelines has two parts. One is an analytical lens that requires analysts to look at what they bring to their work. These include such factors as knowledge, ways of working, information sources and methods, and consultation processes. The analytical lens is reproduced here as a series of questions in Table 5.1. What is important about these questions is that they direct attention to process considerations such as the analyst's own frame of reference and whether those women's groups likely to be affected by the policies have been consulted. A second component requires an exploration of the implications of the policy being analysed according to different factors. Eight factors are identified that represent ways in which discrimination can occur or, conversely, in which equality can be supported. These factors are: (a) legal processes; (b) life experiences; (c) systemic discrimination; (d) economic equality; (e) independence and dignity; (f) violence against women; (g) health and social issues; and (h) social equality. These factors represent content issues that require special attention in the analysis process.

## Table 5.1 A Gender Lens: Analytical Guidelines

| Category | Questions |
|---|---|
| 1. Values Framework | 1.1. What personal and professional experiences, values, and circumstances do I bring to this analysis?<br>1.2. How have I ensured that the diverse experiences, values, and circumstances of individuals and groups who will be affected by my policy issue are reflected in my document? |
| 2. Data and Information Sources | 2.1. Have I considered sources of information other than statistics/quantitative data?<br>2.2. What are my sources for statistics/quantitative data?<br>2.3. Do the statistics used in this analysis include information based on both women's and men's experiences? Are they separated according to gender?<br>2.4. Is there literature or research material on this topic that I should read that presents women's perspectives, experiences, or voices?<br>2.5. Have I considered qualitative data and information? |
| 3. Consultation and Language | 3.1. Have I consulted with women's groups regarding the issue?<br>3.2. If I cannot consult women's groups directly, how have I ensured that their concerns are known and reflected in my analysis?<br>3.3. Have I avoided using language that perpetuates stereotypes?<br>3.4. Is the language used in my document gender-inclusive and respectful of all people? |
| 4. Differences and Diversity | 4.1. Have I considered how women from specific groups, such as women of colour, lesbians, poor women, women with disabilities, and Aboriginal women would be affected by this policy?<br>4.2. Does this policy approach respect cultural and/or other differences?<br>4.3. Does this policy approach consider the needs of women in different regions? Rural and urban? |

Source: 'A Gender Lens: Analytical Guidelines', reprinted with permission from the British Columbia Ministry of Women's Equality.

## An Integrated Model for Policy Analysis

The adoption of a particular lens for analysis focuses on the special impacts of policies with particular groups, and it is our position that policy analysis in the human services must consider whether a special lens should be used to direct attention to such issues as gender and culture. While this focus is essential, the analytical process needs to be located within a more general framework that enables application to a wide range of policy problems. An integrated model that includes both content and process factors and that allows for the incorporation of more specialized considerations within the value-criteria stage is discussed next. This proposed model is accompanied by the following qualifications. First, policy analysis, like policy-making, is not a linear process, and related tasks must be approached with adequate recognition of this fact. Second, supplementary questions or considerations should be incorporated whenever necessary, but particularly in assessing small-scale policies at the organizational level. The proposed model has five steps: (1) problem identification and goal specification; (2) identification of value criteria; (3) assessment of alternatives; (4) feasibility assessment; and (5) recommendations.

## 1. Problem Identification and Goal Specification

The first general step in policy analysis is problem identification and goal specification. Policy analysis really begins with an examination of the problem or need, and several key questions are important to consider. These include the following:

a) What is the nature of the problem?
b) How are the key concepts used to describe the problem defined?
c) Who is experiencing the problem, and what are their characteristics?
d) What social values are being threatened by the problem?
e) Who recognizes that the problem exists?
f) Who defines the condition as a problem?
g) What are the causes of the problem, including relevant theoretical considerations and historical factors?
h) Are there ethnic, gender, and class considerations in identifying the problem?

These questions are similar to those that a policy-maker would ask in assessing needs. However, as noted earlier, a needs assessment should be accompanied by the development of an inventory of strengths and resources, particularly when any new policy is directed at a community or special group. It is also important to identify those likely to be affected by the policy change, how service users are expected to respond to the new policy, and the desired outcome. Relevant actors and interest groups—and the extent of their power and influence—should also be identified at this stage. A related consideration is the salience of the issue. *Issue salience* refers to the ability of the issue to give rise to group action; thus, it is relevant in assessing the potential strength of interest group influence.

In examining an existing policy at the agency or program level, there are some additional questions to consider. These include:

a) What is the basis for policy legitimacy and where does this authority or responsibility lie?
b) Does the desired outcome require system change or system maintenance?
c) What is the level of agreement regarding the policy?
d) What is the nature of linkages between the agency and other relevant systems in the policy environment?

## 2. Identification of Value Criteria

The second general step in policy analysis is the identification of relevant value criteria. The criteria-based model for policy-making encompasses both general criteria and selective criteria specific to the policy issue under consideration. General criteria include questions of adequacy, effectiveness, and efficiency. Effectiveness and efficiency are essential criteria, and efficiency assessment may include strategies such as cost, cost-effectiveness, or benefit-cost analysis. However, as discussed earlier, other considerations must be included in policy analysis within the human services. These include the policy's impact on rights, statuses, and social justice, including the ability of service users to be self-determining. A critical issue is whether or not service users and front-line staff have had opportunities to participate in shaping the policy response under consideration. This participatory element is often omitted from general policy-making models, although, in practice, efforts are sometimes made to elicit some input from these constituencies.

Process models of policy analysis are more likely to address questions of public participation, and this is regarded as an important consideration in policy-making and analysis in the human services. Another important consideration is what Flynn (1992, p. 90) refers to as the SCRAPS test. This test is designed to focus special attention on issues of sexism, classism, racism, ageism, and poverty; the acronym is intended to remind the policy analyst that those who are the victims of such discrimination are likely to receive only 'scraps' without any compensatory attention paid to these issues. During this second step, one can also adopt a special lens that focuses attention on cultural, gender, or other issues. For example, policies that are likely to have a particular impact on women should be assessed by questions emerging from the gender-lens perspective.

The specification of value criteria is included at an early stage in the policy analysis process, although it should be noted that values can also be examined later, particularly in assessing an existing agency policy or in completing a *post hoc* policy analysis study. It must be emphasized that any approach to policy analysis that gives limited attention to values will be incomplete.

It is also important to recognize that the selection of value criteria is not intended to be an arbitrary exercise that allows analysts to impose their particular values on the policy under consideration. Like the conclusions emerging from other types of data, value criteria must be logically defended and justified in order to be accepted as valid. We have argued earlier that policy analysis in the human services imposes a professional responsibility to include criteria that address issues related to social development and social justice. In spite of this ethical obligation, it will be apparent that different criteria or differing interpretations of general criteria can arise. Thus, it is important to provide a specific rationale for the value criteria that are used in completing the analysis. Minimally, this will ensure that underlying values become a more visible component of the policy analysis process; in turn, this will permit more open dialogue and debate about the normative aspects of the policy issue being considered. While we stipulate this as an obligation in an ethical approach to policy analysis, we are aware of the fact that this is often not done. In fact, new policy proposals often contain language designed to obscure rather than clarify underlying values. For example, the language of community partnerships and decentralization is often used to disguise a government's intent to offload service responsibility to community groups and organizations.

## 3. Assessment of Alternatives

The third step in policy analysis involves collecting data on alternatives to be considered in relation to value criteria and the problem analysis and goal selection step. Here one is estimating both the possible anticipated and unanticipated effects of policy alternatives. Both quantitative and qualitative data collection approaches are relevant, and techniques such as forecasting, social indicator analysis, survey research, and other types of program evaluation strategies may be used.

New policies often emerge without adequate attention to the lessons that can be learned from research studies of various aspects of the policy or similar policies adopted elsewhere. This may be a result of strongly held political or ideological beliefs, which lead to little or no attention being paid to the lessons from research. In these circumstances, decision-makers may omit the policy analysis stage of policy development entirely, or use it narrowly to justify a policy decision that has already been made. For example, many critics felt that the federal government's 1996 reforms to Unemployment Insurance followed a process of analysis, including public consultation, that served primarily to justify a decision that had already been made rather than to identify and consider seriously a range of options for policy reform. In cases such as these research studies or consultation processes have little integrity and even less influence. Given this scenario, what are the options? One alternative is to encourage external groups to complete an analysis of such policies. These may provide one or more alternative viewpoints on possible effects. Social Planning Councils, the Canadian Council on Social Development, the Canadian Centre for Policy Alternatives, and the National Council of Welfare are but a few of the organizations that carry out such studies. In particular, the National Council of Welfare is well known for its efforts to include an assessment of the impact of government policies on service users.

At a general level, policy tasks at this point may conclude with a clear identification of anticipated consequences. If policies pertain to agency-level issues or require a careful consideration of service delivery questions, this will be insufficient, however. In such cases, one area of special focus will be the effects of policy change on organizational functioning. Such considerations may include an assessment of the nature of authority, influence, and leadership; patterns of communication; and constraints on policy adoption, including any anticipated resistance to change.

## 4. Feasibility Assessment

Feasibility assessment is identified here as a fourth step in policy analysis. It is included as a separate step because of its particular relevance to analysis in agency- or program-level policies, and its importance to implementation issues. In assessing feasibility, it is important to consider the relative power of the policy. For example, is legal compliance required or is compliance optional? Resource requirements and their availability are also key considerations.

Two other questions may be important. First, does the policy give rise to newly perceived self-interests that need to be considered? For example, new federal legislation on gun control acted as a mobilizing force for the anti-gun-control lobby. In turn, this required the organization of the Coalition For Gun Control, which played a key role in promoting the adoption of this legislation. Second, is there a logical link between policy options and the original problem as defined, including research or theoretical support showing that the intervention is likely to achieve the intended results? This question entails examining whether new policy options are likely to address the problem, and, if so, to what extent.

## 5. Recommendations

The final step in policy analysis involves recommendations that may include support for or criticism of a particular strategy and the specification of anticipated or realized effects of particular policy. The strengths and weaknesses of a limited number of policy options may also be summarized at this point, if the intent is to present a range of options to senior decision-makers for final selection. If this approach is taken, selected alternatives should be considered in relation to value criteria and their ability to address the policy problem.

Table 5.2 summarizes the integrated model for policy analysis. While this model provides only general guidelines for application, it includes elements that encourage connections between the realities of practice and the more general policy questions confronting policy-makers. For example, the identification of key actors and interest groups at the problem-definition step provides information about who is exercising influence at this point in the process. The inclusion of both general and policy-specific value criteria permit the incorporation of elements that may promote increased staff and service user involvement while at the same time answering general questions about effectiveness and efficiency. The inclusion of a feasibility assessment step directs attention to the implementation stage in the policy process; at this stage, the interests of policy-makers and practitioners are most likely to either collide or to coalesce in a new approach to service delivery. The implementation stage of policy-making is considered in more depth in Chapter 6, and an applied example of the integrated model for social policy analysis described in this chapter is included in the Appendix at the back of this book.

## Table 5.2 An Integrated Model for Social Policy Analysis

### Step One: Problem Identification and Goal Specification

1. Problem description: nature and scope.
2. Identification of needs and strengths.
3. Causal factors, including assumptions, theories for explanation, and key historical factors.
4. Targets for change and expected outcomes (goals).
5. Key actors and interest groups that shape problem recognition and definition, including their power and influence.

### Step Two: Identification of Value Criteria

1. General criteria to be considered:
   a) Adequacy
   b) Effectiveness
   c) Efficiency
   d) Impact on rights, statuses, and social justice
   e) Impact on consumer self-determination
   f) Level of staff and consumer involvement
   g) SCRAPS test or application of a special lens
2. Identify selective criteria specific to the policy under consideration, and provide necessary support for their inclusion.

### Step Three: Assessment of Alternatives

1. Identify alternatives to be considered.
2. Collect quantitative and qualitative data on alternatives to be assessed in relation to problem analysis, goal selection, and relevant value criteria.

### Step Four: Feasibility Assessment (especially for agency- or program-level policies)

1. Identify the relative power of the policy, e.g., whether or not it requires legal compliance.
2. Identify the resource requirements and availability.
3. Consider whether the policy gives rise to newly perceived self-interests that need to be considered.
4. Examine whether there is a logical link (theoretical or otherwise) between the policy and the problem or goals initially identified.

### Step Five: Recommendations

1. Evaluate the policy both in relation to intended goals and in relation to the identified means for goal achievement, and/or specify anticipated or actual effects flowing from a particular policy.
2. If requested, summarize the strengths and weaknesses of optional policy choices in relation to problem analysis and value criteria.

## The Role of Research and Evaluation in Policy Analysis

Evaluation was identified as the final stage of the policy-making process in Chapter 4. However, the results of evaluation should be used to make adjustments to all stages of the process, as required. For example, information from the evaluation stage may cause us to alter our understanding of the problem, to modify goals, or to include new activities in the implementation stage. Evaluation, then, is particularly important in policy analysis, and for this reason we position our discussion of evaluation in this chapter.

The use of research to inform policy development is not the rule in Canada, and we have much to learn from the approach that led to the development of the Children Act (1989) in Britain (see Box 5.1).

**Box 5.1** Using Research and Evaluation for Policy Development

The adoption of the Children Act (1989) in Britain is widely recognized as the culmination of a decade-long process that included systematic consideration of research and evaluation findings documenting the effects of various types of social care arrangements on children and their families. This process resulted in legislation that places an increased emphasis on partnerships with parents, even when children are removed from their homes. For example, guardianship options provide for a continuing role for parents whenever feasible, and there is a great deal of emphasis on family visiting and connections while children are in care. New provisions also place increased emphasis on service options designed to support children in their own homes. In addition, service planning now includes more emphasis on the needs of the child and the outcomes that result from the services provided. New systems have been designed to focus attention on these aspects of the case planning process, and resources have been invested to ensure the implementation of these systems within local authorities throughout Britain.

**Box 5.2** Using Policy Research and Evaluation in Policy Analysis

In 1995, the Manitoba Department of Family Services made a policy decision to launch an early intervention program for separating and divorcing parents modelled, in part, on programs first developed in the United States. The three-hour education program, known as *For the Sake of the Children*, provided information on the needs of children experiencing their parents' separation, and it outlined basic strategies to be used in developing a co-operative approach to co-parenting. The program was initially launched as a pilot project with an evaluation component designed to assess implementation and impact, the feasibility of extending the program, and the advisability of making the program mandatory in cases of divorce. The evaluation that was completed provided an assessment of the main effects of this new initiative. The study also identified options, potential consequences, and costs for program extension and expansion. In this case, the evaluation of the program became a key source of information in analysing the future effects of policy-making in this field. Based on the results from this policy study, the program has been extended throughout the province and has been expanded to six hours in order to incorporate additional information and skill-building. (Adapted from McKenzie and Guberman, 1997.)

While the use of government-funded research for policy development is not widespread in Canada, evaluation studies are often commissioned to examine specific policy issues (see the example in Box 5.2). From a provincial perspective, Quebec, more so than other provinces, appears to take a more systematic approach to using evaluation research in policy-making in that it funds studies for this purpose in particular fields of practice, such as child sexual abuse. Furthermore, an important requirement is that these studies involve close collaboration between researchers and practitioners.

At a general level, program or policy evaluation involves systematically collecting, analysing, and reporting information about a program, service, or intervention for use in decision-making. While this identifies evaluation as a technical process, Herman, Morris, and Fitz-Gibbon (1987) note that policy expectations, resources, and other constraints as well as social, organizational, political, and demographic factors significantly affect the process of program evaluation and its impact. These issues blur the lines between tasks within policy and program evaluation in suggesting that both involve activities that are partly social, partly political, and only partly technical. Evaluation in policy-making, then, reflects an action orientation, that is, it is concerned with the adjustment of policy goals, approaches to implementation, or the decision to either extend or terminate a policy.

Program or policy studies make use of methods associated with different approaches to evaluation; Herman, Morris, and Fitz-Gibbon (1987) distinguish between formative and summative approaches. Whereas a formative evaluation examines program or policy processes and is designed to produce information to assist a program in its development, a summative evaluation examines the outcomes, the impact, and the efficiency of a policy.

*Formative evaluations*, sometimes referred to as *process evaluations*, are concerned with the components of a policy or program, what services are being provided, and whether the policy or program is reaching those for whom it was intended. Implementation studies involving an assessment of policy processes are particularly relevant to new policies because they attempt to describe and tease out the details of the policy in order to ascertain what is causing certain effects or whether the policy is being implemented as planned. Two major sets of issues are considered: (1) coverage or actual participation in the program by the intended target population; and (2) service delivery (including the entire sequence of activities undertaken to achieve policy objectives). If a policy or program is not operating effectively, an implementation evaluation can help to determine what has gone wrong and what improvements can be made. Often these problems exist in one or more of the following areas: a) a policy approach or design that fails to meet the needs of service users; b) a lack of program acceptance caused by the attitudes of staff members or administrative policies that create barriers to access; c) program management; and d) program costs (Love, 1992).

*Summative evaluations* concentrate on policy outcomes, impacts, and efficiency. An outcome study is concerned with the extent to which a policy meets its objectives, and, where those objectives involve changes for service users, how long those changes last. Efficiency evaluation is concerned with the ratio of benefits to costs; various forms of cost-utility analysis may be performed, including benefit-cost and cost-effectiveness studies. Box 5.3 summarizes how evaluation has been used to assess program outcomes and costs in a particular policy field, and some of the difficulties that can arise. As this example from the family preservation field demonstrates, a narrow focus on efficiency may divert attention from a more comprehensive review of outcomes. This example also illustrates how multiple evaluations of a new policy may highlight differences in the outcomes that may be experienced during implementation. Two important implications are apparent. First, major policy initiatives that are promoted or adopted on the basis of preliminary evaluation findings may fail to live up to expectations. Second, even when research findings are positive, policy analysis requires us to consider a wide range of studies, assess these results critically, and consider their relevance to our particular policy environment.

## Box 5.3 Assessing Conflicting Results in Policy Evaluation

The conflicting views supported by research and evaluation in policy development are illustrated by reviewing general developments in the field of family preservation. Early research, associated with the Homebuilders Model (a social support program developed in the State of Washington), demonstrated a significant reduction in the number of children in care and related cost savings through the application of a service model stressing short-term intensive services to families in which children were at risk of out-of-home placement. This focus on efficiency and cost-savings led to legislation that mandated such services in the United States, and there was widespread adoption of family preservation programs. In many states different models of service were developed and implemented. More recent evaluations have raised questions about the methods used in early studies and their results. In some cases, family preservation programs have been linked to situations that led to increased risk for some children. However, those studies have also been criticized on methodological grounds, and the debate between advocates and detractors of family preservation as a solution to the high rate of children in out-of-home care continues, with each side identifying somewhat different outcomes as consequences of this policy choice.

Formative and summative approaches to policy evaluation have been discussed as separate strategies; however, most studies combine these approaches. For example, an evaluation may be concerned with both whether the policy is being implemented as intended, and what the effects of the policy are on service users. However, we stress that the evaluation of new policies requires a special focus on formative issues; that is, the activities and the organizational processes associated with implementation. While both quantitative and qualitative methods are relevant to such studies, the collection of data often involves qualitative interviews with key informants, service user feedback, and a review of documents. *Triangulation*, which involves collecting data from more than one source using different data collection methods or different investigators, is recommended in such studies.

An evaluation of a family support program in a child welfare agency (Frankel et al., 1996) illustrates a focus on implementation or process issues and the use of triangulation. Because the policy under examination had been in place for approximately three years, attention was also given to documenting some of the policy's early outcomes. One component of the evaluation involved an examination of service users who had received services over the past eighteen months. A file review was completed, but service contracts that had been signed provided incomplete information on both service activities and outcomes. An interview schedule, which identified various types of service activities and outcomes, was then constructed and pre-tested. The members of the service triad (service user, social worker, and family support worker) were then interviewed to obtain information both on services provided and related outcomes. In addition, outcomes were assessed according to criteria such as the number of children admitted to care, days of care, and current status of the situation. Results from these various activities provided a reasonably accurate picture of the services provided by this program, as well as some information on outcomes. When this information was combined with a pre/post study of current service users that applied several standardized child and family well-being measures, it was possible to provide the agency with a good picture of both implementation processes and the early impact of this family support policy.

A primary focus on outcomes may become the purpose of evaluation in mature programs, and in such studies the use of control or comparison groups can provide additional evidence of whether the policy or program is responsible for observed changes in behaviour or outcomes. In recent years, computer-based monitoring systems that incorporate outcome measures have become quite popular, and such systems have the advantage of providing ongoing feedback to program managers and service providers. While these systems are intended to be helpful, certain disadvantages must be recognized. These systems may not be designed to incorporate feedback from service users, and they usually retrieve and record only quantitative information. Thus, these approaches to evaluation omit the opinions and experiences of service users. In addition, they often fail to promote community and service user empowerment because institutions, such as government agencies, control both the technology and the information.

The evaluation dilemma posed here is not easy to resolve. Information on needs and resources, program design, activities, effectiveness, and cost are essential requirements for good policy-making. Methods for program and policy monitoring as well as carefully designed impact studies can help to provide this information. But these approaches are not sufficient. We argue that such approaches must be accompanied by more participatory methods if we are to generate the kind of evaluation information needed to design programs and policies that respond most effectively to the differing cultural and social needs of service users. While participatory methods are not new, there has been a recent renewal of interest in some of these approaches. One of the authors was involved in a community-based research project that featured two rounds of focus group discussions to launch the process of developing standards of child welfare practice for eight First Nations communities (McKenzie, 1997). Recent books such as *Empowerment Evaluation* (Fetterman, Kaftarian, and Wandersman, 1996) and *Action Research* (Stringer, 1996) outline principles and methods that can be used to promote community and service user control over both the evaluation process and results. Similar issues are raised by Ristock and Pennell (1996), who explore the issue of community research as empowerment within a framework that incorporates both feminist and post-modern perspectives. As well, Health Canada has published a handbook on how stories from service users can be used in health promotion and evaluation (Labonte and Feather, 1996). These approaches to evaluation are valuable because they include the voices of service users. However, to date they have not received sufficient attention by senior policy-makers, including politicians. These individuals often fail to appreciate the results of these studies because the data are regarded as 'soft' or less valid when compared to quantitative information on effectiveness.

To this point we have described policy analysis and evaluation as if all activities were carried out in relation to a single policy. In fact, policy-making often involves the development of several policies embedded within a more general policy direction. This requires the co-ordinated assessment and development of several policies at different levels, often simultaneously. For example, a new general policy in health care designed to integrate community and institutionally-based services is likely to require a new role for hospitals, as well as several new policies that might affect training, utilization, and expenditures within hospitals. For community-based health care services there will also be a number of new policies, such as an increased emphasis on home care, that may emerge from this more general policy change. In circumstances such as these, policy analysis and evaluation must be concerned with the actual or anticipated effects of several different policies. Different methods and sources of data as well as different approaches to analysis should be used in more comprehensive policy studies, and multiple policy recommendations that reflect a more co-ordinated approach to policy development in a particular field of practice is the desired goal. Unfortunately, this more integrated approach to policy evaluation and reform is all too rare in the human services.

Chapter 6 examines the implementation stage in policy-making, and the opportunities that exist at this stage for collaboration between policy-makers and practitioners.

# Implementation: The Interface
# Between Policy and Practice

Implementation is the stage in the policy process when control passes from the policy-makers to practitioners. This is, of course, precisely the reason why policy-makers create a plethora of regulatory policies; they want to ensure that their policies will be implemented as intended. But even the most comprehensive set of regulations cannot prescribe and control all of the actions of practitioners, and the point of no return is reached when policy and procedures manuals become so extensive that they are simply ignored by practitioners. Indeed, one practitioner in child welfare in British Columbia ignored the entire contents of a particularly cumbersome policy manual because the second page included a sentence to the effect that the regulations included in the manual were to be interpreted and used within the discretion of the individual worker. He expanded on the intended interpretation of 'discretion' by concluding that the policy manual itself could be ignored!

## Early Research on Implementation

The implementation stage has received short shrift by policy-makers. Indeed, the policy process has been described as 'front-end driven' in that policy-makers have little time or interest in tracking the fate of legislation once it has been passed. William Greider goes a step further in arguing that many policies are 'hollow' because they represent a public display of action but, without adequate resources, policies cannot attain their objectives (Greider, 1992).

Politicians have not been alone in neglecting implementation. Students of the policy process have displayed an equal lack of interest in what happens following the adoption of a policy, whether this takes the form of legislation or an organizational policy. However, the interest of some researchers was stirred when evaluations of the War on Poverty programs in the United States revealed a notable lack of success in achieving intended outcomes. Indeed, they concluded that many programs had not been implemented as intended, and that implementation is 'the Achilles heel of the policy process' (Williams, 1980).

The publication of a study of urban renewal in the United States (Pressman and Wildavsky, 1973) launched a veritable explosion of research studies on implementation. Having finally discovered implementation, researchers pounced on it, full of optimism that locating the pitfalls in implementation would allow the policy process to unfold in a smooth fashion and policy outcomes to be improved. The early studies followed the lead of Pressman and Wildavsky, who portrayed the essential difficulty as one of control. Particularly in the case of federal policies, implementation difficulties were attributed to two major issues: policies travelled along a lengthy chain of federal, state, and local agencies; and initial policy statements were often vague and open to a variety of interpretations. Pressman and Wildavsky (1973) coined the term 'clearance points', referring to the various points through which a policy had to pass. At these clearance points, policies could be improved, ignored, or sabotaged, thereby allowing state or local officials to alter the original federal intent. The larger the number of clearance points, the greater the potential for altering the policy and its intended effects.

Given this view of the problems of implementation, the solution seemed to lie in stating objectives in a clear and concise fashion, reducing the number of clearance points, and increasing the level of control by federal officials. Clearly this view of implementation was consistent with a top-down and centralized approach to policy-making.

Other early and important studies included *The Missing Link* (Hargrove, 1975) and *The Implementation Game* (Bardach, 1977). The former conceptualized implementation as the missing or forgotten link in the policy process and urged both policy-makers and academics to pay heed to implementation. The latter examined policy-making in the California legislature and asked why some bills became law while others were shunted aside and subsequently forgotten. One reason for the difference was the presence of a 'fixer'—someone who paid attention to the details of the process. Fixers made sure that key legislators were informed about a new Act and, in general, fixers acted as shepherds of the implementation process.

These early interpretations were criticized by researchers who traced the implementation of human service programs. A particularly insightful analysis came from Paul Berman and his colleagues at the Rand Institute based on their studies of the implementation of educational policy (Berman, 1980). Berman distinguished between programmed and adaptive approaches to implementation, arguing that both are appropriate but in different kinds of situations. The essential difference between the two approaches is the extent of change required during the implementation process. Thus, the programmed approach is suitable for policies that can be put into effect in a rather mechanical fashion through the use of rules and regulations. The adaptive approach is required for those policies that must be changed during the process of implementation. The criteria for distinguishing between the two are:

a) the scope of the change;
b) the soundness of the theory or technology behind the change;
c) whether there is agreement on goals among those affected;

d) the degree of control over clearance points;
e) the availability of resources; and
f) the stability of the environment (Berman, 1980).

Berman concluded that an adaptive approach is necessary when any of the following conditions exist: the change is radical and extensive; the theory is tentative; there is little agreement on goals; the degree of control is weak; resources are not readily available; and/or the environment is turbulent. As well, the adaptive approach demanded the active involvement of those responsible for actual implementation. Discretion and interpretation on the part of practitioners are not viewed as problems but as an essential element of the process. It is our view that the adaptive approach is most appropriate in the human services, especially in fields such as health care and child welfare.

Berman's work prompted a number of scholars to develop criteria for effective implementation. The rationale behind these inquiries was that if criteria could be developed and tested, then guidelines for successful implementation could be specified in a prescriptive, top-down fashion by policy-makers. One set of criteria that was developed included the following items:

a)  clear and consistent objectives;
b)  adequate causal theory;
c)  implementation process legally structured to enhance compliance by implementing officials and target groups;
d)  committed and skilful implementing officials;
e)  support of interest groups; and
f)  changes in socioeconomic conditions that do not substantially undermine political support or causal theory. (Sabatier, 1986, pp. 24–5)

The above list is by no means the most comprehensive. From his largely successful experience as the administrator of health services in New York City from 1967 to 1983, Gordon Chase identified fifteen criteria and forty-four factors that are required for effective implementation:

A framework is presented for examining obstacles to the implementation of human service delivery programs. These obstacles arise from three sources: the operational demands required by the new policy, the nature and availability of resources and the need to share resources with other actors. Within these broad categories fifteen areas deserve special attention, including the people to be served, the nature of the service, the likelihood of distortions, the controllability of the program, money, personnel, space and the intersection with senior agencies, special interest groups, politicians and other affected interest groups. By searching each of these fifteen areas diligently with the aid of some 44 factors for consideration it appears possible to make relatively powerful predictions about the obstacles to be encountered. (Chase, 1979, p. 216)

Chase's list of obstacles is so daunting that one wonders how his agency got past the analysis stage. But even the more modest requirements proposed by Sabatier are rarely present, and too often there is inadequate support from committed and skilful implementing officials. Indeed, as a second group of researchers pointed out (Lipsky, 1980; Williams, 1980), human service practitioners who are responsible for implementation may be skilful but not necessarily committed to new policies. One reason is that these new policies may be seen as unnecessary and as adding to an already crowded plate of responsibilities. We turn now to a brief review of the bottom-up approach to implementation.

From their examination of the implementation of manpower and educational policies, Williams and Elmore concluded that local delivery units, whether social service agencies, schools, or public health offices, determine whether policies will be changed, sabotaged, or implemented as intended. Their research revealed that human service organizations are:

> bottom heavy and loosely coupled. They are bottom heavy because the closer we get to the bottom the closer we get to the factors that have the greatest effect on the program's success or failure. They are loosely coupled because the ability of one level of the organization to control the behaviour of another is weak. (Elmore, 1979a, p. 27)

Given these organizational characteristics and given that policies in the human services often require changes to meet local conditions, the logical conclusion is that 'the serious business of implementation consists not so much of finding new ways of controlling and regulating the behaviour of subordinates, but of enhancing the capacity of the local delivery unit' (Elmore, 1979b, pp. 215–16). In a similar vein, Williams argued that:

> the main message of the implementation perspective is that the central focus of policy should be on the point of service delivery. . . . After the 'big' decisions get made at the highest levels, what is done by those who implement and operate programs and projects has the critical impact on evolving policy. (Williams, 1980, p. 5)

Based on these conclusions, Elmore argued for a 'backward-mapping' approach to policy-making in which policy begins with practitioners. 'The closer one is to the source of the problem, the greater is one's ability to influence it; and the problem-solving ability of complex systems depends not on hierarchical control but on maximizing discretion at the point where the problem is most immediate' (Elmore, 1982, p. 21). However, despite the potential of a backward-mapping approach, neither Elmore nor other scholars in implementation developed the notion into a practical guide for policy implementation.

The conclusions of Williams, Elmore, and others placed a spotlight on a neglected aspect of implementation: the capacity and motivation of practitioners to implement policies they had no opportunity to shape. Indeed, as we noted above, practitioners often regard new policies imposed from above with suspicion if not downright hostility.

To a considerable degree the early research on implementation yielded a number of suggestions for improving the policy process. The first was to make the process cleaner by reducing the number of clearance points. A second argued for a tight system of control to ensure that practitioners could not deviate from the intent of the policy. A third, derived from Berman, called for identifying the kind of policy being implemented and then carefully matching implementation strategies to the policy. Fourth, Elmore's backward-mapping strategy argued that, in the last analysis, successful implementation remains in the hands of staff in local community offices. Accordingly, improvements are most likely to be found in strengthening the capacity of these local-level units to deliver programs. A fifth suggestion, advocated by Sabatier (1986), Yanow (1987), and others, called for a synthesis between top-down and bottom-up approaches through the development of policy communities.

## Implementation and the Impact on Practice

Given that the participation of practitioners is an integral part of backward mapping and policy communities, we need to consider the potential of practitioners to contribute to the policy process. Are practitioners interested in and capable of participation? What constraints hamper them? We begin by reviewing a number of studies: an investigation of the work patterns of street-level bureaucrats in Boston in the 1970s (Lipsky, 1980); research pertaining to the quality of work life of nurses and child welfare workers in British Columbia in the early 1990s (Attridge and Callahan, 1990); an implementation evaluation of British Columbia's Corrections Branch (Wharf, 1984); and a study of the work environment of child welfare workers under regionalization in Winnipeg (McKenzie, 1989). While we acknowledge that these are limited sources, they nevertheless provide a basis for some tentative conclusions about the involvement of practitioners in the policy process.

Our discussion of practitioner involvement recognizes the organizational context presented earlier, when we argued that practitioners are often oppressed by their work environments and by the corporate approach to management that dominates these environments. This argument receives considerable support from the research that led to Lipsky's (1980) theory of street-level bureaucracy, a theory that explains why committed professionals become alienated and disillusioned within those bureaucracies that provide service to involuntary clients.

The street-level bureaucrats studied by Lipsky were a mixed lot. Lipsky does not identify the organizations from which they came, and it is difficult to know if the social work population in the study were child welfare workers or staff members in a public welfare department responsible for social assistance. These street-level bureaucrats also included police officers, teachers, and lawyers in storefront legal aid offices. A common characteristic is that these professionals work in the most difficult of circumstances; they are insufficient in numbers to provide the services needed, they lack the resources to respond adequately to the needs of those receiving services, and they confront crises on a daily basis. They work with people who are poor, who live in inadequate housing, if not on skid row, and who are stressed by a range of personal troubles and public issues. As Lipsky noted:

> street-level bureaucrats spend their work lives in a corrupted world of service. They believe themselves to be doing the best they can under adverse circumstances and they develop techniques to salvage service within the limits imposed upon them by the structure of their work. At best street-level bureaucrats invent benign modes of mass processing that more or less permit them to deal with the public fairly, appropriately and successfully. At worst they give in to favouritism, stereotyping and routinizing. (Lipsky, 1980, p. xiii)

The image presented in *Street-Level Bureaucracy* reminds us of TV shows like *Hill Street Blues* and *NYPD*. In these shows the 'consumers' are depicted as losers, mired in a life of crime, callous toward others, including friends and relatives, and addicted to alcohol and drugs. Faced with this group of 'clients', the police often resort to unacceptable modes of conduct: they treat people with disdain, and they regard other street-level bureaucrats, such as public defenders and social workers, with amused contempt. We suggest that staff of public welfare departments and of hospital emergency rooms in large urban centres invent similar ways of dealing with disreputable individuals.

To say the least, Lipsky's conclusions reveal a depressing portrait of the world of human service workers and the people they serve. His central conclusion is of primary importance to the discussion here: from the perspective of the individual receiving service, the street-level bureaucrat or the front-line worker makes policy. 'The decisions of street-level bureaucrats, the routines they establish and the devices they invent to cope with their uncertainties and work pressures, effectively become the public policies they carry out' (Lipsky, 1980, p. xii). The point is that if these workers are as oppressed as Lipsky claims, then their capacity to participate in and contribute effectively to a backward-mapping approach to policy-making is significantly constrained.

A second source of information comes from a study of the role of probation officers in policy-making in the Corrections Branch in British Columbia (Wharf, 1984). Despite efforts by senior management to create structures that involved probation officers and local supervisors in the development of policy, the vast majority of probation officers reported that they had little or no influence in developing and changing Branch policy. The typical view of probation officers was that 'policy comes from head office to regulate and control our practice' (Wharf, 1984, p. 24). Policy was seen as removed from the realities of practice, and, furthermore, policy manuals and the constant revisions to procedures were greeted with scepticism, if not outright derision.

By far the most active participants in policy development were counsellors in family court. These people occupied relatively new positions in the Branch and, unlike in other areas of responsibility, policy had to be established rather than changed and adapted. The lesson from this study seemed clear: in situations in which there is an opportunity to create new policy, the invitation to contribute is more likely to be accepted than in situations in which policy and procedures are well established.

The research of Attridge and Callahan (1990) into the quality of work life of nurses and child welfare workers yielded some important insights. The scarcity of resources and the demands of the organizations in which they worked were not dissimilar to conditions experienced by Lipsky's street-level bureaucrats, and the workers defined themselves as oppressed, just like the street-level bureaucrats described in Lipsky's book. However, a more positive picture emerged; when nurses and child welfare workers could escape from completing endless forms and reacting to crises and could instead spend time with the people they serve, listening to them, respecting them, and working out plans together, a feeling of true professional accomplishment emerged. What accounts for the apparently different outcomes? One explanation may lie in the differences between the policy and organizational environment of British Columbia compared to that in a large urban centre in the United States. In addition, workers in the BC study probably had had more professional training than most of the street-level bureaucrats in Lipsky's research.

A positive response by street-level bureaucrats was also identified in McKenzie's study (1989) of child welfare workers in Winnipeg's decentralized system. A stressful work environment—the primary variable affecting the response of street-level bureaucrats—certainly existed within Winnipeg's child welfare system at the time of this study. For example, new agencies established in 1985 were plagued by conflicting goals, particularly in relation to protection and prevention. As well, inadequate resources coupled with increased service demand had resulted in heavier workloads and therefore greater stress for staff. Under these conditions, Lipsky had argued, feelings of alienation intensify. In order to maintain a reasonable degree of job discretion—as well as a sense of the ability of practitioners to influence their work environment—or control over that environment, staff feel compelled to adopt routine and stereotypic ways of processing people. In effect, these accommodations by workers partly explain the slippage between idealized policy goals and actions at the street level.

McKenzie's study was designed to test Lipsky's propositions empirically. Information on job stress, alienation, job discretion, and the tendency to adopt stereotypic behaviours toward people being served was collected from 167 front-line child welfare workers. While reduced job discretion was associated with an increase in feelings of alienation and a tendency to express stereotypic attitudes, these relationships were not particularly strong. Moreover, there was little support for the predicted relationship between job stress, identified by Lipsky as a key variable, on other behaviours, including the adoption of routine and stereotypic ways of dealing with service users. Despite high levels of job stress, staff also expressed a relatively high degree of satisfaction with both the new policy of service decentralization and their sense of accomplishment on the job. These findings suggest that the relationship between job stress on other behaviours is less deterministic than Lipsky's theory would have us believe, although it must be recognized that this survey was conducted only two years after the creation of new community-based agencies.

While caution must be exercised in interpreting these results, two important conclusions can be drawn. First, high job stress does not always lead to a reduction in job discretion and to adverse consequences for people being served. To a certain extent, the presence of job discretion may counteract the effects of high workload demands and mitigate the adoption of more routine approaches to 'people-processing'. Second, street-level bureaucrats are not simply passive respondents to bureaucratic characteristics; rather, some practitioners challenge, change, or ignore the rules and regulations confronting them.

Despite the doom and gloom scenarios provided by Lipsky and by the Corrections Branch study, some staff can and will contribute to the policy process if they are given the opportunity and the resources to do so. In particular, opportunities to contribute must involve work on a meaningful project or on issues important to staff. A common form of so-called 'participation' involves an invitation to respond to policies that have been drafted in head offices. At best, such token participation takes the form of consultation rather than genuine partnership. Meaningful participation is less likely when it involves an invitation to respond to policies drafted by officials for whom there is already considerable commitment to these policies.

Can any lessons be learned from these examples and the literature on implementation? We suggest that the examples provide general support for Lipsky's (1980) and Yanow's (1987) conclusions that gaps between policy and practice should be expected as a normal outcome of the differences in values and priorities between policy-makers and practitioners. Even when objectives are clear, when resources are available, when the environment is stable, and when there are few clearance points, the process of implementation will often alter the intended policy. Indeed, implementation is a powerful but usually neglected stage in the policy process. It is this stage that fundamentally alters objectives and intentions; indeed, at the point at which policy becomes practice, it will almost invariably be changed. Policy will either be ignored, as in the case of the child welfare worker in BC when faced with unhelpful policy manuals, or it will be altered. The issue, then, is not so much whether implementation will alter policies but whether these alterations will improve or weaken programs and services. Moreover, the question becomes whether we can build in processes to ensure that the implementation stage is characterized by improvements rather than impediments to service.

As researchers on implementation have acknowledged, '. . . concentration on implementation has added little to our theoretical understanding of policy-making beyond the fundamental idea that implementation cannot be taken for granted in a complex policy-making environment' (Linder and Peters, 1987, p. 460). Yet even this insight shatters the myth of the 'textbook' model of the policy process that is so prominent in many books on policy-making. In addition, implementation studies, particularly the work of Williams and Elmore, have identified the crucial importance of the local-level delivery unit in determining how policy will be implemented. But Elmore's challenge that improvements to policy-making and implementation require the involvement of practitioners as well as the allocation of additional resources to local offices where implementation occurs, has, to date, been largely ignored.

## Future Directions

What might be done to ensure that the domains of practice and policy are more closely connected? We begin by noting the conclusions of a study that reviewed attempts to introduce innovations into social work practice in the United Kingdom. The study concluded that despite all the efforts to improve services through such structural reforms as integrating health and social services and altering the geographic boundaries of organizations, practice did not change (Smale, 1996). When everything around them is shifting, practitioners cling to their one constant—their practice and their day-to-day interaction with the people with whom they work. The insight derived from this study and from the work of many scholars in implementation is clear: improving practice requires that practitioners must be centrally involved in the change process. What might practitioners bring to this process?

Practitioners would argue with some passion that they often feel like those they serve—poorly paid, unappreciated, and oppressed. Any significant attempt to change practice must address these perceptions. Take, for example, the issue of salary. Supervisors in local child welfare offices have many years of experience, they set the tone of the office, and they influence the quality of practice in a most significant fashion. Yet these individuals receive about half the salary of senior bureaucrats in central office. There are compelling reasons to argue that as *the crucial players* in the child welfare enterprise, they should be paid as much as people at the policy-making level.

While the issue of income equity may be difficult to address in the near future, other initiatives would be much easier to implement. Indeed, it is difficult to understand why provincial ministries and other human service organizations do not provide increased access to continuing education and conferences on a regular and routine basis. Another relatively simple change would involve collecting and publishing examples of effective practice, and providing easy access to available research in the field. In relation to the latter issue, several local authorities in Britain have set up computer terminals so that summaries of practice-based research studies, including guidelines for implementation and evaluation, can be easily accessed by staff.

More difficult changes include providing sabbaticals for practitioners with many years of service and shifting personnel between local and head offices. As difficult as these changes may be in the current fiscal climate, they would reassure practitioners that they are valued, as well as providing them with opportunities for advanced training and professional development. One concrete example of the potential benefits of enhanced respect for personnel is a recent arrangement by the Ministry for Children and Families in British Columbia, along with a number of Schools of Social Work, to establish a condensed BSW program for experienced workers who lack this degree. While some workers were at first reluctant to return to school, most have found it a rewarding and challenging experience. One worker about to complete the program indicated to ministry officials that the program had reaffirmed his commitment to child welfare. If he had not been given the opportunity to return to school, the worker admitted that he would not have stayed much longer in the ministry. The costs in both monetary and service terms of replacing an experienced worker far exceeds the costs of attending to the educational needs of staff. Indeed, one of the long-standing problems in all jurisdictions in child welfare is staff turnover. Slowing down the turnover rate would have enormous advantages for both staff and those being served.

However, paying attention to and valuing staff might still leave them on the margins of policy-making. Including practitioners in policy-making is extraordinarily difficult in large organizations. Indeed, we suggest that organizations like provincial ministries are inhospitable places for programs such as child welfare, and in Chapter 9 we argue the case for community governance in these types of services. In small organizations, staff know each other, they know the challenges facing others in the agency, and they can swap positions so that all staff come to understand all aspects of the work to be done.

Even in large organizations some creative ways can be found to involve practitioners and service recipients in policy-making. One way is to establish policy groups consisting of representatives from each level of the organization as well as from the service user population. Such vertical-slice groups can meet on a regular basis to develop and review policies, thus providing a vehicle for putting backward-mapping into practice. For example, groups might develop risk assessment procedures that are anchored in the day-to-day experience of staff and of service users. Such policy groups might review whether risk assessment procedures are required in all situations of neglect and abuse. Can risk assessment be done in a way that respects and involves service users? Is there or should there be a place for service users to sign off the risk assessment form to indicate their approval of the assessment and the plan for change? More fundamentally, should risk assessments be replaced by approaches to practice that focus on strengths rather than deficits? Such policy groups might suggest family action plans that incorporate a consideration of risks but that place these risks alongside the capacities and resources of families (Weller and Wharf, 1995).

Policy groups might also argue for more control over the work of local offices. For example, offices typically have little discretion over budgets and service users have to be squeezed into programs in order to receive assistance. One telling comment on the rigidities of program budgets was made by a service user in BC: 'What I need is a bus pass; what I am offered is a parenting program that I don't need and can't get to anyway' (Callahan, Hooper, and Wharf, 1998). It might well be that a global budget controlled by the local office would be much more appropriate both for practitioners and for service users.

In suggesting the establishment of policy groups consisting of representatives from all levels of the organization and from those who receive service, we are aware that practitioners and those they serve might be overwhelmed at first by the sophistication of the policy process. Matters such as how to construct budgets or how to develop submissions to the Treasury Board or to Cabinet might produce feelings of inadequacy on the part of those unfamiliar with the required procedures. As noted in earlier chapters, the literature on citizen participation is unanimous in concluding that for the most part only middle- and upper-class individuals participate. It is possible to overcome such difficulties such as these, however, by establishing training sessions on effective participation prior to engaging in the activities of a policy group.

A classic example of implementation gone wrong and one that illustrates the difficulties typically encountered in top-down approaches comes from the experience of implementing the recommendations of the Gove Inquiry into Child Protection in British Columbia. The inquiry investigated the circumstances surrounding the death of four-year-old Matthew Vaudreuil at the hands of his mother. For most of his life Matthew lived in a small, northern community. His mother, a young single parent beset by a number of problems, including poverty and a fragile sense of self, received services from a plethora of agencies. The array of 'helpers' consisted of child care workers, nurses, social workers, homemakers, physicians, and mental health counsellors. The sheer number of these people and the lack of connections among them served to hinder rather than to ensure the provision of effective assistance.

The inquiry sought to remedy the lack of co-ordinated and integrated services by recommending that all services for children, youth, and families be centralized in a Ministry for Children and Families. A transition team headed by a former deputy minister of education was established to implement this and many other recommendations emerging from the inquiry. The team's report calling for a new ministry was approved by the provincial government. The Ministry for Children and Families now includes mental health services; probation, and drug- and alcohol-related services for youth; as well as public health and child welfare services.

The restructuring required to integrate these previously separate programs and services has entailed dissolving old staff positions and creating new ones, recruiting and hiring staff for these positions, establishing new geographic boundaries, relocating offices, installing integrated information and reporting systems, and, most fundamentally, developing a common philosophy among staff. All of these changes have occurred within a climate of fiscal restraint and at a time when the number of children in care has risen, thus substantially increasing the costs of foster care.

As is readily apparent, the changes have been comprehensive and unsettling. Nevertheless, the ultimate goal of improving the quality of service is far from accomplished. Indeed, long-serving staff members report that they have never felt so confused, alienated, and overworked. One clear indication of poor staff morale occurred in November 1997 when the entire social work complement of a local office in Quesnel went on stress leave, protesting their complete inability to cope with 'caseloads' of sixty to seventy service users.

One alternative to an integration of services imposed in a top-down manner would have been to employ a modified backward-mapping approach to implementing this particular recommendation made by the inquiry. Such an approach would have required the ministry to first set out policy guidelines at the provincial level for the integration of services, and then to invite regional managers and their staff to develop plans suited to the communities in each region. As we note in Chapter 9 on community governance, this approach would have resulted in different patterns among communities, but a diversified pattern would not only permit communities to develop a unique model of integration but would also foster a sense of ownership by the communities. In addition, tracking the consequences of a diversified pattern of integration would have allowed for some effective comparisons between models.

The above suggestions are consistent with the literature on implementation that argues for backward mapping or a synthesis of top-down and bottom-up approaches. These suggestions assume that the domains of practice and policy can be brought closer together. An opposing view is that senior policy-makers believe that the participation of practitioners and service users is neither practical nor desirable. In a recent conversation with one of the authors, a senior bureaucrat claimed that the two domains cannot be connected in large organizations, and that the only remedy for connecting policy and practice is to create smaller, more community-based organizations. In addition, all approaches to connecting practice and policy require policy-makers to surrender some of their power, an unlikely scenario for those individuals who are dedicated to acquiring rather than relinquishing power. If this is the reality, at least in some policy environments, are there any other ways to improve practice?

While few practitioner/service-user alliances have been established, we argue the case for these alliances in Chapter 10, particularly in circumstances in which senior planners foster an élitist approach to the policy-making process.

# Part 2

## Toward an Inclusive Paradigm in Policy-Making

# Shared Decision-Making: A Case Study

STEPHEN OWEN

## The Case for a Shared Decision-Making Model

British Columbia is Canada's third largest province, with a population of approximately 3.7 million people living in an area larger than France and Germany combined. Approximately 93 per cent of the province's area is publicly owned land. Featuring rainforests, subarctic areas, mountains, and deserts, BC is a biologically diverse province, with 280 mammal species, 500 bird species, 85 freshwater fish species, 21 amphibian species, and 17 reptile species. Coniferous forest covers most of the land area, and for almost a century the forest industry has been the driving force behind the provincial economy. British Columbia accounts for 35 per cent of world softwood lumber exports and 10 per cent of the world's newsprint exports. Mining, fishing, and, increasingly, tourism also contribute significantly to the province's economic growth.

The 1980s were a period of bitter conflict over the use of forest lands. Various groups protested forestry practices such as clear cutting and the impact of logging on values such as biodiversity, fish and wildlife habitat, water quality, and scenic landscapes, as well as on the sustainability of timber supplies. The traditional belief that British Columbia had an apparently limitless supply of natural resources was challenged by the demands of a growing and increasingly mobile population. Technological advances in the forest industry in recent decades had enabled companies to increase the amount of timber taken from the forests, while at the same time reducing the number of jobs per unit of timber cut—a matter of considerable concern to workers during the mid-1980s recession. Thus, there were growing concerns about the sustainability of forestry-dependent community economies, environmental values, and the way of life of communities depending almost wholly on the forest industry. These concerns were combined with a growing recognition of the interdependence of economic, environmental, and social needs, reflected at a global level in the 1987 World Commission on Environment and Development report (the Brundtland report), which noted an urgent need for all nations to promote sustainable development.

The conflict during the 1980s acted as a catalyst for debate about the future of the forest industry in particular, and of land use and resource management in British Columbia in general. One result of the debate was the identification—by the government-appointed Forest Resources Commission, by the Round Table on the Environment and the Economy, and by others—of the province's need to develop a comprehensive land use strategy to balance and integrate all values and achieve the long-term objective of economic, environmental, and social sustainability.

The government of British Columbia responded to these concerns in 1992 by establishing the Commission on Resource and Environment (CORE) with a legislative mandate to develop and oversee the implementation of a provincial land use strategy and to facilitate the development of strategic regional land use plans.

The need for a comprehensive provincial land use strategy is related to the more general dysfunction that confronts society in the processes and substance of public policy decision-making. The dysfunction expresses itself in a widespread public cynicism about government effectiveness and fairness, and in the resulting dissatisfaction with the actions and decisions of government.

In a land use context, the current procedural dysfunction is demonstrated by the rejection of the results of planning processes. Parties from across the spectrum of interests in land use regularly attempt to do 'end runs' around decisions reached by processes in which they have played no meaningful part. The Chief Forester reduces the allowable annual cut of a corporate timber licensee and the company seeks judicial review; a permit is issued for a logging road into an undeveloped watershed and an environmental group resorts to civil disobedience and sets up a blockade; Cabinet ministers are lobbied by various interest groups against administrative land use decisions; and media campaigns—often spiced with exaggerated claims—are launched at home and abroad. A common tendency is for government to react to these end runs with *ad hoc* decisions unrelated to formal planning processes, often because of pressures for early decisions. This creates inconsistency and enhances public distrust and alienation.

Significant land use dysfunction exists in British Columbia, notwithstanding an apparent abundance of natural resources and environmental splendour. The province continues to suffer significant debt, unemployment, and internal conflict, even though, with a population of less than four million, it enjoys a massive state-owned land base and resource-lode. This dysfunction expresses itself in the ongoing loss of environmental options, resource jobs, community stability, and business certainty. It has become widely understood that such continuing losses can be halted only through the application of land use principles of broad sustainability. It is clear that social stability will only be achieved through economic strength, which can only be maintained through environmental integrity. Achieving balanced land use decisions that respect this interdependence can only be achieved realistically through the development of a broad consensus.

In summary, the general dysfunction in society reflected in the lack of widespread public support for government decisions, especially in matters of resource and environmental management, needs to be addressed through decision-making processes based on the meaningful participation of all significantly affected interests, and substantive results that are based, as far as possible, on principles of broad sustainability.

## The Work of the Commission on Resources and Environment

CORE identified five components essential to the development of a sustainable land use strategy:

1. A clear government vision of sustainability, expressed through principles set out in a Land Use Charter,[1] and through a legislative and policy framework;
2. Meaningful public participation, emphasizing consensus-seeking processes in the development of land use and resource management plans, to encourage stable and sustainable land uses that balance a range of values;
3. Careful co-ordination among all government agencies involved in resource and environmental management;
4. A comprehensive, consistent, and accessible system for the resolution of disputes and of appeals against decisions; and
5. Independent monitoring of the progress of the strategy toward achieving sustainability.[2]

In 1992, the government of British Columbia also directed CORE to address land use conflicts in the four most controversial regions of the province over an 18-month period: Vancouver Island (3,000,000 ha), Cariboo-Chilcotin (8,000,000 ha), East Kootenay (4,000,000 ha), and West Kootenay/Boundary (4,000,000 ha). The key challenge was to develop a participation process that would enable strongly opposed and politically influential public interest groups to try to reconcile their differences in a manner that would permit the government to act decisively on many highly controversial land use issues. CORE proposed round-table-style negotiations ('shared decision-making') in which all affected parties would participate in the development of regional land use plans that would identify new protected areas as well as other zones. This approach was adopted by the interest groups in all four regions as well as several local pilot projects. Regional round-table participants defined their own sectors of interest, designed their negotiation process, and proceeded to build as much agreement as possible, given the time and resources available. Government participated directly in the negotiations. CORE provided logistical support, mediation services, and training in interest-based negotiations.

None of the regional round tables was able to reach agreement on all issues in the time provided; however, substantial progress, including many sub-agreements, was achieved in all cases. After their negotiations adjourned, CORE recommended land use plans for each of the regions based on the agreements reached and the information gathered through the round-table negotiations. Subsequent negotiation between the government and the affected groups adjusted the CORE recommendations and positioned the government to make decisions regarding the use of areas that had been impossible for previous governments to deal with decisively. By the spring of 1995 the government had made comprehensive land use decisions for all of the CORE regions, just two-and-a-half years after CORE began its work. At the same time the shared decision-making process developed and tested by CORE was refined and adapted to serve as the principle means for facilitating public participation and consensus-building in land use planning in the remaining areas of the province.

## The Lessons and Limitations of Public Participation

### Operationalizing Shared Decision-Making in a Public Policy Context

Representative government can be supplemented effectively with greater public participation by drawing on the best of both direct democracy and sectoral interest negotiation. The key is that such participation must be open, so as to be responsible; balanced, so as to be fair; and advisory, so as to entrust decision-making with accountable, elected officials. An effective example is the 'shared decision-making' processes pioneered in British Columbia to negotiate long-term, sustainable uses of public forests and other natural resources.

Shared decision-making means that on a certain set of issues for a specified time, those with authority to make a decision and those affected by that decision are empowered jointly to seek an outcome that accommodates rather than compromises the interests of all concerned. Parties distinguish between their interests and their demands or positions that fail to take into account the needs of others. Because different groups will value different things, clear self-analysis, communication, and understanding of others' interests can lead to a package solution that provides better outcomes for each party than if the groups were simply competing on their own.

One example of shared decision-making in British Columbia concerns the issue of timber harvesting. Broadly stated, the interests of environmentalists are to protect biodiversity and to ensure that other non-timber values such as visual quality, recreational use, and aesthetics are sustained. Labour interests want secure employment, rural communities want economic diversification and stability, and corporate interests want certainty of return on investment. Shared decision-making can lead to all-gain solutions where more sensitive harvesting techniques encourage greater employment through forest restoration projects and smaller-scale operations; a more diversified rural economy through protection of fish stocks and tourism values; and corporate certainty through land use zoning and the reliable supply of timber.

Not every shared decision-making process will result in a full consensus resolution. Much depends on external factors, such as a guiding government policy framework, relevant information, and sufficient time and resources to support the process. However, policy, information, and resources alone are insufficient to get the job done. At least as much depends on the collective will of the participants to create opportunities for innovative outcomes that are not possible for any participant acting alone. Where one or more see themselves, or are seen by others, as being able to get what they want independently, progress will be slow.

When full agreement cannot be reached, the efforts of the participants can still enrich the decision-making process by clearly defining problems, narrowing the scope of issues, and identifying a range of possible alternatives for resolution. Whether or not the participants come to terms, the building of working relationships and mutual understanding among the participants will help ensure better outcomes.

Participating effectively in such public policy negotiations requires that the participants receive very specific orientation in a new process for communicating and working with each other. In turn, the application of the newly learned process enables substantive learning to take place through collaboration and interaction over time. These skills are learned through:

- analysing one's self-interest;
- articulating this analysis to those with different interests, perspectives, and needs;
- listening to others' articulation of their interests;
- jointly identifying fundamental principles;
- developing new analytical tools for measuring the advance of one's own interest and the overall impact of alternative solutions;
- defining a common problem; and
- collaboratively designing all-gain solutions through an interactive process of proposing, debating, analysing possible impacts of, and comparing alternatives.

Shared decision-making draws on as broad a range as possible of perspectives, interests, and experiences to help government develop and implement public policy. It can supplement traditional representative government by closing the gap between those making decisions and those most affected by them, and by directly addressing the feeling of alienation that is a major dysfunctional force in conventional decision-making processes.

In public policy negotiation, where the fullest range of interests are effectively represented in a balanced process, the consensus reached should be politically irresistible to government, even without any formal devolution of decision-making authority. However, not achieving consensus on every issue is not a failure. Through a process that brings a fuller range of interests, better information, comparative analysis, and substantive learning to the participants and those they are advising, better decisions will almost inevitably result. Such decisions will be more balanced, better informed, and more stable because they have involved those who are most interested in, knowledgeable about, and affected by the outcomes. The relationships developed among the competing interests through the shared decision-making process promote stability. This stability results from the balanced, collaborative nature of the process and from the new relationships that enhance understanding and respect and promote flexible adjustments in light of new information and experience. This sustaining process therefore contributes to a sustainable result.

### Shared Decision-Making as Mutual Learning

The learning process for participants in shared decision-making tends to be irreversible in that it develops understanding and respect for other perspectives. It also introduces a powerful tool for understanding one's own interests and how best to achieve them through co-operation with others. Despite high levels of continuing conflict and dissatisfaction, those who participated in CORE's large-scale shared decision-making processes continue to speak in 'interest-based' terms and insist that the processes be maintained during implementation of the regional plans, local-level planning, and monitoring by citizens.

The shared decision-making approach provides a powerful motivation to learn about one's own self-interest through careful analysis of alternative processes (litigation, civil disobedience, lobbying, media campaigns). This approach also entails learning about the interests of others who can either advance or block one's own interests. This not only leads to better 'all-gain' results, but it also has the potential to promote strong relationships among previously competing groups.

This approach to public policy development requires a certain level of readiness on the part of all participants, including government. The mandate of the process should be clearly defined and placed within a policy and fiscal framework that directs the parties toward a realistic solution. The process also requires information, technical and administrative support, and thorough pre-negotiation assessment to ensure that all the necessary parties want to and can take part effectively.

Notwithstanding the ideals of readiness, it is important not to be too rigid. The learning nature of the shared decision-making process means that both substantive policy and procedural rules can be improved by the interaction that takes place. For example, the CORE Vancouver Island negotiations were unable to reach consensus largely due to the absence of an economic transition policy from government. However, this very absence caused the negotiation process to develop and deliver to government a detailed, balanced, and highly practical transition strategy that was later adopted by the government in the implementation of the final plan through Forest Renewal BC. Similarly, the process and procedural rules simply had to be negotiated and improved through trial and error across a range of negotiating processes because of the parties' mistrust of each other and of those in authority, and their resulting insistence that they run their own show. This learning process has now created a body of experience in the province that can serve convincingly as a standard model for any new negotiations.

One conceptual aspect to readiness is that there must be a general acceptance by all interests of the need for change and of the interdependence of each interest in obtaining the best result. Often, this conclusion cannot be reached in the absence of a clear message from government that change will occur with or without one's participation. Alternatively, circumstances may have deteriorated to the extent that the need for change is obvious to all.

While all interested parties must see a negotiated approach as their best alternative, it is likely that different groups will be at different stages of readiness and in a better or worse position to participate effectively. In this situation, it is necessary for the convening or facilitating body (CORE in the BC case) to proactively ensure balanced participation. This task can frustrate the facilitator if the objective is interpreted as bias rather than balance by those who are losing their previous economic or political advantage.

Another challenge to readiness can arise when the pathology of conflict within the situation is so great that the parties' mistrust of each other leads to negotiated process rules that hamstring the ability to reach a consensus solution. This happened in the CORE Cariboo-Chilcotin negotiations; the decision-making rules required full consensus on the whole package covering every issue, without which all ideas, scenarios, and strategies had to be abandoned. As a result, the participants reached agreement on many issues that were later abandoned because of lack of agreement on a total package. While this result might have been avoided if the facilitator had introduced a more flexible set of process rules, the pre-existing level of mistrust might have led to a rejection and immediate collapse of the process anyway. Ultimately, the situation had to play itself out as a learning experience.

The tension between perfect readiness at the outset, achieved only through top-down imposition of process rules, and the messiness of 'learning as you go' can challenge the political resolve of government to support shared decision-making processes through a period of learning and change. However, even with the high levels of conflict and dissatisfaction and the failure to reach consensus in the initial CORE processes, the public seems most disinclined to reduce its demand for the right to participate directly in major public policy decisions.

Readiness is an issue both at the outset of a negotiation process and throughout the process. Learning takes time, and the time required varies for different participants. In British Columbia, the perceived urgency for completion of regional land use plans led government to place arbitrary limits on the duration of negotiation processes—an average of approximately 18 months. Thus, learning (and the opportunity to reach consensus) may have been constrained by the requirement to conform to pre-set deadlines.

Shared decision-making does not mean that parties must compromise or sacrifice their fundamental interests and values. Rather, it means that they should distinguish these interests and values from their demands or positions that fail to take into account the needs of others. While conflict can be debilitating, it can also be a creative force if it induces an enriching variety of perspectives, broader understanding, and balanced and synergistic results through collaboration. Also, the very crisis that can lead to an acceptance of a new approach by all interests should challenge each party to carefully examine its underlying assumptions, values, and beliefs against the reality of better information and new ideas to see if adjustments are appropriate. Examples in the forestry dispute include re-calculating the long-term sustainability of current harvest levels; and the need for total protection of wilderness compared to the alternative of less protection and effective management for all values across the whole landscape through a new Forest Practices Code.

As noted above, conflict can be either debilitating or creative. Shared decision-making asserts that parties to a public dispute do not have to abandon their key values. However, the crisis leading to a participative approach should cause all parties to reconsider and perhaps temper what they view as bedrock principles in light of new understanding of other perspectives and needs and the clear inadequacy of the status quo that is generating the conflict. It is healthy to challenge our 'first principles' regularly against other legitimate points of view, new information, and continuing experience in order to either renew our faith or make realistic adjustments. To do so effectively involves an intense learning experience.

Fundamental to the prospect of learning in shared decision-making processes is respect for the other parties and bargaining in good faith. CORE has developed a code of conduct[3] to guide these processes to this end, but a key role for the mediator or facilitator is to ensure respect and an opportunity for balanced and effective participation for all. Effective collaborative results will occur only if parties are willing to learn from each other. Learning will only take place through the willingness of all to understand and articulate their own interests honestly, and to listen to and understand others.

In shared decision-making, there must be a clear understanding from the outset as to the roles and responsibilities of all parties, including government and non-government participants. This includes the recognition that the role of the participants is advisory vis-à-vis the lawful government decision-maker, but that a consensus decision will be implemented to the greatest extent possible by government. This assumes that government is represented corporately as one of the parties to the negotiation and that it is informing the other participants of policy and fiscal constraints. When no consensus is reached, a default procedure to government—including, in the British Columbia case, the preparation and publication of a public report by CORE—must be clearly understood from the outset. A major threat to such processes will occur if government is not sincere in its desire to involve and listen to a full range of public interests in the development of public policy. Objectives, expectations, and a code of conduct should be explicit at the outset and the whole shared decision-making process should be transparent to ensure a positive result, with or without consensus.

Such transparency will ensure congruence between the espoused theory of public participation and how the theory actually plays out in practice. To encourage good-faith bargaining by all, government must discourage parties from making 'end runs' around the process through direct lobbying of ministers. The learning that is necessary to support a successful shared decision-making process requires a certain amount of wary trust. This is particularly difficult when it is most needed, for example, in a process that responds to a demand for greater public participation arising out of strong feelings of alienation, cynicism, and conflict. However, when expectations are raised and not met, a major backlash will result from those who feel betrayed by government.

Learning requires testing beliefs and assumptions against new information and ideas. While this can involve risk, desperate situations involving the obvious need for change can override reluctance to take a risk. That being said, a learning process will likely be more successful when protections against the threats to fundamental interests of the parties are incorporated.

## Managing Risks

In the CORE public negotiations, the need for protective margins provided by a government policy framework was evident. For example, it was very difficult for labour leaders to publicly negotiate new protected areas that could lead to a decrease in timber harvest, and therefore jobs, without an economic transition strategy that would increase employment intensity and opportunity through other means. Also, it was difficult for environmentalists to accept fewer areas of total protection without a strict Forest Practices Code showing that the full range of non-timber values could be protected outside parks through the enforcement of higher harvesting standards. And forest companies would not willingly accept reduced harvesting areas without knowing what compensation policy would apply to lost harvesting rights and without the long-term certainty of permanently designated harvesting areas. The lack of clear policy in all of these areas made public negotiations toward consensus difficult in the first round. Yet the clear direction to government concerning the issues and details to be expressed in provincial policy came from the negotiation processes themselves. Again, the interactive nature of top-down policy with bottom-up participatory direction contributes to effective public policy change, development, and implementation.

The risks of participation in public negotiations can also be managed if parties do not abandon alternative opportunities to get their own way. These can include government lobbying, media campaigns, threatened market boycotts, and lawsuits. While good-faith bargaining requires the suspension of these activities, parties will probably and appropriately keep their options open as a defence against the risks of the public negotiation process. Moreover, as parties realistically assess their options, they often discover that significantly higher risks accompany their alternatives to negotiation. CORE's experience has been that the parties often overestimate what they can achieve through force of will. Mediators can expand the margin for learning by encouraging parties to engage in 'sober second thought' with respect to their alternatives.

The imbalance of resources affects the margin of risk and therefore the relative power that parties may perceive in entering into public negotiations. An essential role of the facilitator is to ensure that power is balanced as much as possible through sharing of information, financial assistance for participants, and procedural rules.

Government officials also face risk in entering into public shared decision-making negotiations; they may fear that their statutory authority is being reduced. This fear can be overcome by demonstrating the empowering nature of consensus decision-making in delivering to the statutory decision-makers creative, integrated, and widely supported solutions. This must be compared to the weak nature of command-and-control decision-making processes. Professional development, interest negotiation orientation, and cultural change within government bureaucracies are necessary to reduce this feeling of risk.

During a shared decision-making process, procedural safeguards such as straw polls (i.e., unofficial polls), package deals, and access to more accurate and neutrally obtained data can reduce risk. In this regard, incrementalism in building agreement over time can be much more effective than an 'all or nothing' agreement at the end of the day, as was required in the CORE Cariboo-Chilcotin negotiations. Risk can also be reduced by neutrally obtained information and clearly understood and well-supported analytical tools to measure the impact of various scenarios. In the CORE regional negotiations, the development of a land use designation system, multiple accounts analysis methodology, sectoral interest statements, and maps enhanced confidence in the learning process. The shared decision-making process will identify areas of common interest or areas where interests are valued differently and can be traded within a package solution. This is particularly important when the various interests are all legitimate, compelling, apparently competing, and yet interdependent. As such, no group can fulfil its interests without the support of others, and the collaborative approach of interest negotiation provides the opportunity to balance respective, different priorities within a package solution.

When there is a clear crisis, the status quo cannot be maintained, and there is a need to manage change, the incentive to take a risk may bring all parties to the negotiating table. This will only occur, however, if government makes it clear that that is 'where the action is', and that a failure to take part will pose the greater risk of not having an opportunity to influence the outcome. This was a fundamentally important factor in the relative success of the CORE negotiations. In particular, the motivation on the part of traditional political and economic power-brokers to negotiate with those without political power relies on a clear message from government that the rules are changing, and that all participants need the support of others to get what they want.

Sustainability cannot be imposed from above because it must be informed in a balanced and ongoing way by the widest spectrum of interests and perspectives. However, the uncertainty and messiness of this dynamism is also its major strength, because it is likely to be more realistic and flexible in responding to unforeseen circumstances and new information over time.

### Shared Decision-Making as Shared Planning

There is a superficial attractiveness to logical, sequential, strategic planning, beginning with the top-down development of principles and goals, followed by a clear and comprehensive policy framework and detailed inventories and technical support mechanisms. In theory, these are then combined with broad-based and balanced public participation processes. However, this is not the way the political world works, nor a likely context for effective learning. The CORE experience—an attempt to develop and implement integrated and sustainable, social, economic, and environmental policy—shows that the urgency of a situation can demand that everything proceed at once—principle and goal development, policy framework, information and technical support, and public participation. While this approach can produce frustration, prolong conflict, and threaten political resolve, it also allows interest groups to inform and learn from all others, resulting in a more resilient, comprehensive, and often unexpected result.

Public participation in policy development and implementation promotes self-analysis, communication, and creative synergies, all of which are major stimulants to learning and achieving more balanced, more stable, and wiser decisions, whether or not full consensus is achieved. This new process is one of dynamic research in which attitudes and ideas are tested, first against other perspectives and in the context of increasing information, and, second, against the experience of implementation. Especially when the process takes place under the imperative of a changing and threatening environment, new attitudes, values, relationships, and solutions will be developed.

The CORE experience indicates that even in the case of considerable consensus agreement, as in the East Kootenay negotiations, an impasse will eventually occur beyond which further agreement is not possible. It is important to acknowledge the progress that has been made, and that the balance of interests and the new information, ideas, and options passed on to the statutory decision-maker will lead to better decisions. Up to the point of total impasse, however, the CORE experience has shown that various options for moving the process beyond obstacles are possible. These include the referral of matters to technical working groups, third-party arbitration, parties standing aside rather than withholding consensus, the development of a range of options, and voting. With respect to voting, it should be understood that simple majority votes will be less persuasive and certainly not considered binding by the decision-maker.

The Vancouver Island and Cariboo-Chilcotin CORE processes concluded without adopting major policies such as an economic transition strategy to provide the margin of safety for rural communities and resource workers, and no definition around Protected Area Strategy boundaries and percentages. The negotiations were time-limited and simply had to be concluded at that point. Missing policies were then formulated, based on ideas that arose during negotiations. These were included in the CORE reports as recommendations, and were later adopted by government.

A key aspect of public interest negotiation is that each party must fully analyse its Best Alternative to a Negotiated Agreement (BATNA)[4] and retain the right to withdraw from the process if it feels it can better serve its interests outside the process. If these processes are to produce considerable consensus and to see their decisions implemented, then it is important for government to understand that it can affect the various parties' BATNAs through its policy development and rejection of lobbying initiatives outside the process.

A major lesson for all parties from the CORE regional processes is that the status quo was unsustainable; that change was occurring and would be managed through the development and implementation of integrated and sustainable social, economic, and environmental policies expressed within a comprehensive regional strategic plan; and that all interested parties were to take part in negotiating the plan. However, with or without consensus, at the end of the day CORE would be responsible for developing and publishing a recommended strategic plan and government would make a final decision on it. In retrospect, it is clear that some parties did not believe that this would happen and thought that they could either maintain the status quo or influence a plan tilted to their advantage by withholding consensus or acting outside the planning process. Government actions in approving and giving legal status to the strategic plans have shown this not to be the case; this will be a significant precedent for all interested parties in subsequent processes.

By every indicator of change, including percentages of different land use designations, management objectives and guidelines, economic transition and diversification strategies, provincial policy recommendations, and implementation strategies, both the CORE recommendations and the subsequent government plans in all four regions are a major departure from the status quo in terms of sustainable resource and environmental management. While some differences of land use designations occurred between the CORE recommendations and the government plans, they are almost identical in terms of sustainability principles, balance, strategic policies, and resource strategies. The similarity between the CORE recommendations and the approved government plans is best appreciated by comparing either of these to the status quo, which demonstrates the extent to which a new paradigm has been introduced.

Procedurally, the new levels of meaningful public participation introduced through the CORE processes have also been adopted by the participants and government through various community processes. These processes are to:

- oversee the implementation of regional plans;
- advise government on local resource planning;

- participate in economic transition initiatives;
- provide a community link to Aboriginal treaty negotiations; and
- advise government agencies on a range of social, economic, and environmental sustainability issues.

Another important lesson from the CORE public participation experience relates to the role of professionals and technical advisors in the processes. Each negotiating table had a team of government technical advisors assigned to it from a range of government agencies. This approach meant that the government experts had to work as an integrated team, mostly for the first time. In doing so, they had to subordinate their individual ministry mandates to support the objective of the process to develop collaborative and balanced solutions. In addition, their demonstrated competence and diligence gained the respect of the wide range of participants from different sectors, enhancing the credibility of government in the eyes of the public. Furthermore, throughout the process, the government officials gained a respect for the volunteer efforts, the wisdom, and the different perspectives brought to the process by members of the public and came to appreciate the value of public participation as an empowering force for government rather than as a threat to their authority.

Achieving sustainability through the implementation of integrated social, economic, and environmental policy is a highly dynamic undertaking. The CORE experience shows that it is a continuous process of public involvement at the local level; impact monitoring through the development and measurement of sustainability indicators; monitoring and enforcement of standards; public review and reporting; and amendment of policies and plans to respond to ongoing experience. This is an adaptive management approach whereby permits and approvals to resource users are issued on a performance basis.

Sustainability is a process as well as a product. It is based on balancing social, economic, and environmental principles and integrated goals. These often compete with each other and therefore must be reconciled through highly participatory planning and then subjected to a continuous process of dynamic measurement and adjustment. Public interest negotiation leads to informed, balanced, and stable decisions, yet also provides flexibility to respond to new information and experience because of the understanding and respect developed among the parties.

Ambiguity can arise between the development of policies and plans and their implementation. In the CORE experience this ambiguity sometimes assisted in mobilizing constituency support within a wide range of interest sectors behind an emerging consensus in order to give the plan time to demonstrate its effectiveness. However, great care must be taken to ensure that any existing ambiguity is not promoted as a matter of bad faith so as to discredit the process and the result. The fact is, however, that ambiguity is inherent in sustainability planning in the face of rapid and threatening change and many unknown factors.

Incentives offered by government to motivate adoption of sustainability plans have proven to be not only helpful but also essential in the CORE processes. If well managed, the Forest Renewal Plan, drawing on large financial resources made available through increases in the public rent on public land timber harvesting, has the potential to provide for forest rehabilitation, increased and diversified employment, value-added manufacturing, intensive forest management, and research and development, all of which provide the motivation for a wide range of interests to support transition to sustainability. Enlightened self-interest is not necessarily inconsistent with good public policy.

The success of implementation of a sustainable land use plan must be measured against the integrated principles and goals and not by the letter of the agreement or plan. Ongoing experience and new information will always change the details, but should not change the need for a balanced and participatory approach.

A major challenge in the CORE regional planning processes was to ensure that a major cross-section of the public had an opportunity to participate in a meaningful way. This meant helping to organize interest sectors that could be represented in an accountable way at the public negotiation sessions. Another challenge (often not met), of the initial CORE processes was to keep the sector constituencies and the general community informed about the process and involved in guiding the results. It became clear that greater effort and resources are necessary to ensure that this constituency and community participation takes place in an effective way.

A major difficulty in the large-scale CORE regional planning processes was that many of the sectors were not natural constituencies over such large geographic areas, and thus had difficulty in keeping those they purported to speak for involved. However, this challenge must be balanced against the value of breaking down organized interest group intransigence by forming sectors with broad rather than narrow perspectives. A further complication was that even though the negotiating sessions were held in communities throughout each region on a regular basis, the often detailed and tedious nature of land use planning failed to catch ongoing community attention even when public sessions were held in their midst.

In response to this experience, CORE developed a Code of Conduct[5] with specific recommendations for accountability and communication of sector representatives to their constituencies, as well as communication responsibilities for the whole negotiation process vis-à-vis the general community. The West Kootenay-Boundary and East Kootenay CORE processes, extrapolating from the previously concluded Vancouver Island and Cariboo-Chilcotin processes, took their table reports to openhouses in communities throughout each of their regions before CORE prepared its final recommendations for government consideration. Subsequent strategic planning sessions are proceeding on a smaller geographic scale where sector constituencies already exist, thus enhancing communication. The proposed community resource boards are expected to be standing volunteer bodies that will develop a close relationship with the general community on a range of issues over time.[6]

Public participation through multi-sector public interest negotiation is an essential component in management for sustainability. Such negotiation not only enables government to obtain comprehensive and balanced information needed for the development and integration of economic, social, and environmental policy, but also encourages the stability of integrated policy that is perceived to be rooted in and to reflect the broad public interest. By encouraging conflicting interests to understand and reconcile their differences, the process also builds good will and resilience within communities. This is in stark contrast to consultative models that can exaggerate the differences among conflicting interests as participants adopt extreme positions in the hope that a compromise decision will be in their favour.

## Conclusion

The CORE experience has been an interesting episode in the recent history of land use planning and sustainability in British Columbia, which includes the BC Round Table on the Environment and the Economy, the Forest Resources Commission, and the ongoing work of the Land Use Co-ordination Office and Environmental Assessment Office inside government. Throughout its operations, CORE stimulated intense debate and controversy as it addressed its statutory responsibility to lead, change, and balance social, environmental, and economic interests through intense public debate, negotiation, and planning. It was this catalytic role and the emotions it stirred that led, perhaps inevitably, to CORE's demise in 1996. CORE was created by the provincial government as a challenge to itself and to the public to embrace uncomfortable but essential change. Having unsettled established practices and influences and mobilized a broader range of interests in the decision-making process, CORE provoked strong reactions. Yet CORE's arousal of this often-heated reaction allowed the provincial government to broker final land use agreements and support for policy changes which, while closely resembling the proposed CORE plans and recommendations, were one step safely removed from the heat of the public, multi-party negotiations.

It was appropriate that the lead land use planning function be reassumed within government following the developmental phase of CORE. Government works best when it assumes responsibilities directly and delivers services in an unambiguous and accountable way. Independent commissions can be useful in stimulating change but are not as accountable in delivering basic public services on a permanent basis, compared to government agencies.

However, a major gap remains in the provincial land use and sustainability strategy with the discontinuance of CORE: an independent monitoring agency with investigative and public reporting responsibilities. This need is amplified by the reduction in federal and provincial programs for state of environment and sustainability study and reporting.

The achievement of sustainability will require long-term commitment and vigilance. Like the national debt, it is an issue about which we cannot afford to become complacent, either in British Columbia or in any other part of the world. British Columbia, unlike many other jurisdictions, is in the enviable position of having both a strong economy and a relatively intact natural environment. Along with the opportunity to act, the province also has a responsibility to act. Each of the above and other related initiatives is an important component in the gradual achievement of economic, environmental, and social sustainability, which combine to form a promising beginning to a permanent commitment.

# A Policy Community:
# Developing Guardianship Legislation

DEBORAH RUTMAN

## Introduction and Context

This chapter relates the story of the development of the adult guardianship legislation in British Columbia in the early 1990s. It describes a legislative development process without precedent in British Columbia or in Canada. The story tells of the formation and ongoing activities of a coalition of individuals and community groups across BC who worked with government representatives to shape and ultimately draft four interrelated Acts. As a participant observer of this process, I will first recount this story as I understood and experienced it, and then I will discuss some key issues based on my observations and reflections. This chapter departs from the format of other chapters, given my personal and, at times, intense involvement in the process.

At the time I viewed this development as an example of partnership between government and community. Although this view remains valid, it is also clear in retrospect that the partnership illustrates the activities of a policy community as introduced in Chapter 2. This policy community was responsible for the initiation and development stages of the policy process.

Adult guardianship legislation concerns the laws and procedures surrounding the appointment of a substitute decision-maker for an adult who has been deemed incapable of making decisions on his or her own behalf. Those affected by the guardianship legislation include:

a) adults with a mental handicap, mental illness, severe physical disability, or head injury;
b) adults who have experienced a stroke or have a degenerative disease such as Alzheimer's Disease, Parkinson's Disease, Huntington's Disease, or AIDS; and
c) citizens who may experience diminishing capacity in the future.

Clearly, given that any person could become incapacitated at any time through injury or illness, this legislation is extremely important, and could potentially affect any one of us.

In British Columbia, guardianship legislation—the Patients Property Act (1960)—had been in existence for over thirty-five years, and people who had applied it argued that it was not very appropriate or useful. Major long-standing criticisms of the Patients Property Act included the following: it pertained to financial decision-making only and contained no provision for health care or personal care decisions; it provided no option to pre-plan; there was no recognition of the assistance and support provided by family and friends or the notion of natural advocacy; and, perhaps most important-ly, the court process mandated in the Act was demeaning, demoralizing, inflexible, time-consuming, and expensive.

By the late 1980s, the time was ripe for British Columbia to begin review-ing its guardianship legislation. Besides the need to address the above criti-cisms of the Patients Property Act, a number of additional factors set the stage for reform. Among these were:

a) The de-institutionalization movement of the 1980s, which involved both a shift in social attitudes toward community support and the recognition that from an economic perspective institutionalization was not sustainable.

b) The launching of the 1986–7 justice reform process, which involved a number of community hearings. These hearings resulted in an out-pouring of criticism about BC's existing guardianship legislation, as well as complaints from community groups, self-advocates, and fam-ily members about the inaccessibility and bureaucracy of the Office of the Public Trustee.

c) The appointment of a new Public Trustee in BC in 1989. The new Public Trustee, Myrna Hall, was committed to widescale reform and to community involvement in the reform process.

d) The review of guardianship legislation in other jurisdictions in Canada, most recently in Ontario, as well as in Australia and New Zealand.

e) The review and planned overhaul of related legislation in BC, most notably, the Mental Health Act and the Family and Child Service Act.

f) The launching of the Royal Commission on Health Care and Costs, and, along with it, the trend in government toward community con-sultation processes.

In sum, by 1989, it was evident that BC's adult guardianship legislation would be reviewed with an eye toward legislative reform. There was a con-fluence of political, social, and personal commitment to change, and to com-munity involvement in the change process. To use Kingdon's terms, prob-lems, policies, and politics converged to open the policy window (Kingdon, 1995). The primary outstanding question concerned the process by which legislative reform should unfold.

## The Process of Legislative Change

### Early Development

In 1989, the then Executive Director of the BC Association for Community Living invited a number of interested individuals and representatives of community organizations to come together to talk about BC's existing guardianship legislation. Among those involved in these discussions were people with developmental disabilities, people with major mental illnesses, and people with degenerative illnesses, as well as the caregivers/advocates for all these individuals. Participants shared their experiences with regard to the existing legislation (the Patients Property Act) and concluded that the legislation and its accompanying policies and practices had generally failed to meet their needs. While participants had differing ideas about how to rectify the situation, they were in agreement that legislative reform was necessary, and that reform efforts needed to honour the experiences and recommendations of those most personally affected by the legislation.

As an outcome of these discussions, five community organizations sought joint funding from the Law Foundation for a project to review adult guardianship legislation in British Columbia. The project, called the Project to Review Adult Guardianship (it came to be known by its acronym PRAG), was sponsored by the BC Association for Community Living and was based at the Community Legal Assistance Society. The project received funding from the Law Foundation in 1989. Over the course of three years, the number of people involved with PRAG grew from a handful to 3,000, and the number of organizations involved grew from five to 300.

The funding obtained from the Law Foundation enabled the group to carry out a community-based action research project. The PRAG researchers undertook a province-wide survey to canvass views regarding the existing legislation and proposed directions for reform. This initial survey promoted widespread community awareness of the issues and ultimately built a community-wide coalition: '(T)he questionnaire generated broader interest and expanded membership in the coalition. It became an education tool bringing us all up to speed in the difficulties with the current legislation' (Etmanski, 1992, p. 1). This process led to an 'awakening' of interest among community members in undertaking a major community engagement process and creating a diverse community-based coalition focused on law reform. Fuelled by the enthusiastic response to its initial survey and intent on extending its community engagement work, in 1990 PRAG applied for and received a major grant from the Law Foundation and from the Notary Foundation of British Columbia.

Shortly after the formation of PRAG, the Office of the Public Trustee was prompted by the 1987 law reform process to spearhead the creation of an Inter-Ministerial Committee on Issues Affecting Dependent Adults. The Inter-Ministerial Committee's mandate was to examine and ultimately undertake guardianship law reform. The Committee comprised fourteen government representatives from the ministries of the Attorney General, Health, and Social Services. Thus, in 1989, the establishment of PRAG and the Inter-Ministerial Committee on Issues Affecting Dependent Adults meant that two separate legislative review processes were underway in British Columbia.

The parallel and potentially disconnected nature of these review process-es gave rise to some concern in early 1990, especially among senior policy-makers. Their response was to select a small number of community leaders within PRAG to serve as 'advisors' to the government's law reform process. PRAG was unwilling, however, to settle for 'advisory' status for two main rea-sons: first, because this would quell the momentum of the community's own coalition-building and legislative review activities; and second, because PRAG saw itself as an equal partner with government in the legislative reform process. From PRAG members' perspective, the impetus to launch legislative reform work had come largely from the community; as well, initial public consultation activities had been undertaken by the community and had been funded by non-government grants. Perhaps most importantly, community members, having experiential knowledge of the existing legislation, saw themselves as being in the best position to both critique this legislation and to inform the law reform process.

PRAG members took their arguments to senior bureaucrats within the Ministry of the Attorney General, and convinced the deputy minister that the final products of the guardianship law reform process would be signifi-cantly enriched by the information generated through PRAG's community consultation initiatives. Moreover, PRAG convinced the deputy minister to lengthen the government's timelines for the reform process by approximate-ly one year, thereby synchronizing the timeline with PRAG's own estimates of a timeline for their community consultation processes. Through these early meetings with senior bureaucrats, PRAG both demonstrated its credibility and registered its expectations in relation to its collaboration with government. This could be seen as the first 'test' of the 'equal partnership' approach to legislative reform, and PRAG members were both pleased and possibly (secretly) a bit surprised by the outcome.

In 1990, the Project to Review Adult Guardianship and the Inter-Ministerial Committee on Issues Affecting Dependent Adults came together and agreed to set down a joint Letter of Understanding, which outlined the groups' respective and collaborative activities. It was agreed that the groups would join in reforming British Columbia's adult guardianship legislation and related regulations, policies, and procedures. The scope of activities ranged from examining the definition, role, and organization of advocacy and com-munity supports/services, to identifying the provisions for formal substitute decision-making/guardianship for adults. The work was to be shared and divided such that each partner of the coalition—government and communi-ty—undertook activities in keeping with its respective strengths: the commu-nity coalition was to undertake extensive consultations with approximately 3,000 people in BC to set the directions for legislative reform, and the gov-ernment was to write policy papers, complete cost analyses, and so forth.

PRAG's province-wide community consultation, and its draft of discussion papers sent to over 1,300 people to review and critique culminated in the production of a 'Framework Document' in July 1991. Although it needed refinement and elaboration in many places, the document was a landmark in that it contained the project's statement of its vision of the guiding values and principles for new adult guardianship legislation. The inclusion of guiding principles would eventually be a major hallmark of the guardianship legislation. The document also contained directions for new legislation and for policy.

The challenge of arriving at a common set of guiding principles for the new legislation must be emphasized, given that adult guardianship inherently brings into consideration two fundamental—and for some, opposing—social values: the right to self-determination of the individual; and the right to protection for vulnerable persons. In view of the number and diversity of constituencies comprising PRAG, including people with head injuries, adults with developmental disabilities, and the caregivers of all these people, differences in perspectives regarding guiding values and principles were extremely strong at times. In particular, tensions arose between those who advocated for policy solutions that focused on providing personal support and assistance so as to maximize individual autonomy, and those who favoured approaches that focused on adult protection. According to Etmanski (1992), discussions and debates regarding core values and principles took countless hours, but the result, which was based on group consensus, significantly strengthened the community coalition.

### Establishment of the Joint Working Committee: Fall 1991

PRAG's initial Framework Document was presented to the Ministry of the Attorney General for review in July 1991. Interestingly, it seemed as though the Inter-Ministerial Committee had been waiting for the Framework Document in order to use it as a base for its legislative reform work. As the next step in the process, PRAG and the Inter-Ministerial Committee formed a joint committee to continue discussion and debate in relation to reform of the adult guardianship legislation. The mandate of the Joint Working Committee was to 'synthesize government and community perspectives on adult guardianship issues, and to clarify, refine and add depth to the Framework Document' (Etmanski, 1992, p. 2).

To accomplish the objectives of the Joint Working Committee, another extensive consultation process was undertaken. Citizens and groups were invited to provide the Joint Working Committee with written and verbal responses regarding the Framework Document. As well, members of the Joint Working Committee met with groups across British Columbia and obtained feedback on the document. In addition, the Committee made use of the work of PRAG's seven existing task groups, which continued to meet in order to discuss complex issues in critical content areas, such as consent to health care, abuse and neglect, and the assessment of capacity.

After an intense, ten-month collaborative effort, the final version of the Framework Document was jointly written by a government-community team. The document was entitled *How Can We Help? A New Look at Self-Determination, Interdependence, Substitute Decision-making and Guardianship in BC.* It was submitted to Cabinet in September 1992 as a policy document to be used in framing the drafting of the new guardianship legislation. Cabinet accepted the Framework Document, and the attorney general made a commitment to introduce new guardianship legislation based on *How Can We Help?* by the spring of 1993.

### Legislative Drafting and Policy Planning: Fall 1992–Spring 1993
In order for legislation to be introduced in the spring 1993 session of the Legislature, legislative drafting needed to commence by the fall of 1992. The question of what would become of the partnership, and of the community's involvement in legislative framing, was now crucial. While the degree of community involvement in legislative development was already unprecedented, the notion of active community participation in legislative drafting was foreign to many in government.

According to Etmanski (1993), by the fall of 1992, when the final version of *How Can We Help?* was ready for legislative drafting, government was ready to revert to its former style of working with community—that is, by meeting with an extremely small and select group of community members who would be said to 'represent' a broad community voice, or by striking a community advisory committee.

From the community's perspective, the government's plan to continue working with only a handful of PRAG members ran counter to the community's principles and work processes to date. The government's intention to limit its dealings to the four community members comprising the Joint Working Committee was antithetical to the inclusive and participatory nature of the community coalition. As in the past, the community was not willing to stifle the energy and momentum that had developed over the past three years, or to 'retire' the hundreds of volunteers who had spent countless hours contributing their time to task groups and committees.

In response, PRAG opted for the political strategy of negotiating with government regarding the community's involvement in the legislative drafting and policy development process. Given the election in 1991 of a new provincial NDP government and its stated commitment to community participation in policy review, PRAG members had reason to hope that senior bureaucrats would be receptive to the idea of working in tandem with government on legislative drafting. Members of PRAG met with the attorney general and obtained his support in relation to two precedent-setting plans: first, there would be a joint community-government legislative drafting team; and second, government and community would establish a number of joint government-community policy committees.

Based on this agreement, the new guardianship legislation was drafted by a three-person team (two from government, one from the community). At the same time, six community-government policy groups, each composed of five community and five government representatives, were formed. Their mandate was to review relevant sections of *How Can We Help?* in order to provide recommendations to the Joint Working Committee regarding legislative drafting instructions and/or policy and implementation issues. Finally, and also importantly, the membership and terms of reference for the Joint Working Committee were renegotiated so that a community representative from the policy groups was added to the Committee's membership. From PRAG's perspective, the expanded Joint Working Committee, and the participation of numerous community members in the policy groups, signalled ongoing community ownership of the legislative drafting process, as well as improved accountability on the part of government to the community constituencies.

The legislative drafting and policy planning work during this eight-month period was fast-paced and intense; arguably, this was the most frenetic period of the legislative development process to date. The legislative drafters and Joint Working Committee met weekly; the community representatives on these groups reported back to PRAG's working committees as frequently; and the policy groups met one half-day per week for up to three months, with participants spending many additional hours researching and discussing potential policy options. Everyone was acutely aware of the tight timelines for writing the new legislation; at the same time, PRAG members were committed to information-sharing and consensus decision-making within the community coalition—time-consuming work, to be sure.

### Community-based Legislative Response Committees: Spring 1993

By early spring of 1993, drafting of the new legislation was well underway. While the community coalition was already fully involved in the process, PRAG requested the establishment of a number of community-based legislative review committees. The proposed 'Terms of Reference' for these groups were to synthesize responses to the legislation and to prepare a report for the attorney general and the Joint Working Committee with recommendations for amendments to the new legislation and/or proposals for policy.

The Joint Working Committee agreed that Legislative Response Committees would be 'helpful in channelling diverse reactions to the legislation and in maintaining one voice through first reading of the legislation in the House' (Gabelmann, 1993). As a result, in yet another precedent-setting move, seven Legislative Response Committees were formed: one to review each of the four Acts comprising the guardianship legislation, and three additional 'theme' groups to examine how the new legislative package addressed pivotal, overarching issues such as advocacy and the assessment of capacity. Thus, Legislative Response Committees would have access to, and would comment upon, the draft legislation prior to its introduction in the Legislative Assembly.

Each of the Legislative Response Committees consisted of at least one community-based lawyer and one person from the community with no legal training; both had participated in either a policy group or in PRAG's ongoing working groups. A total of twenty people were involved in reviewing the legislation, representing a variety of community and professional interests, as well as expertise in the area of adult guardianship. In undertaking their work, the Committees went back to *How Can We Help?* to ensure that the essence of the Framework Document was reflected in the draft legislation.

Through May and June of 1993, the Legislative Response Committees worked at a breakneck pace to review the draft legislation and to prepare a report proposing amendments. The reports were submitted first to PRAG, then, with PRAG's endorsement, to the Joint Working Committee, and then, ultimately, to the attorney general. The ministry received the committee's report at the end of June 1993 during second reading of the guardianship legislation in the legislature (the period during which the principles of the bills are first discussed, and then the articles within the bills are debated, section by section).

As a result of the Legislative Response Committees' work, ninety-three changes were made to the guardianship legislative package. Moreover, in a letter to the chair of the Legislative Response Committee, the attorney general voiced his appreciation for the monumental work undertaken by the Committee:

> I want to express my sincere appreciation to your Committee members for their extraordinary effort in reviewing the proposed legislation. Your report has allowed the government to bring further clarity and completeness to the legislative package. . . . Thank you for the excellent analysis provided by your Committee, and I look forward to the establishment of the joint implementation process. (Gabelmann, 1993)

At long last, after an extensive, often arduous, and ground-breaking four-year collaborative process, the adult guardianship legislative package was passed by the Legislative Assembly in July of 1993 (see the Appendix to this chapter for an overview of the principles and components of the new legislation). The package has been heralded by many within both government and the community as the best and most innovative legislative framework in North America. The process of its development and passage—the process of community-driven legislative reform—is certainly just as unique.

### A Postscript: Summer 1993—Winter 1997–8—Waiting for Proclamation

Though passed in the legislature in the summer of 1993, as of the winter of 1997–8 the guardianship legislation has yet to be proclaimed. At one point, the legislation was slated to be proclaimed in the fall of 1996, but that year came and went without proclamation. Why? While it is beyond the scope of this chapter to analyse in depth the possible reasons for this delay, it cannot conclude without speculating about possible key factors contributing to this evident impasse regarding the legislation's proclamation and implementation.

In hindsight, perhaps it is not surprising that the road to implementation and proclamation has been, and inevitably would have been, bumpy. Arguably, at least two key issues affecting the bumpiness of the process were evident even in 1993: the nature of the government-community partnership again needed to be resolved, this time in relation to implementation activities; and the community energy had ebbed—it needed to find ways to recharge itself physically, emotionally, and financially. These two factors are discussed below, along with several additional ones (that perhaps were not evident in 1993), that appeared to affect the ultimate fate of the legislation.

### Government-community partnerships
In the summer of 1993, following the passage of the new legislation, the community coalition clearly continued to hold strong expectations regarding its involvement in implementation processes. Many community members appreciated how crucial the implementation period was, and that PRAG's tremendous work to date could be dashed if implementation activities were not well planned and well executed. The provincial government also spoke of continuing its collaborative relations with the community during implementation, as was evident in the earlier cited letter from the attorney general to PRAG. Nevertheless, many key members of PRAG sensed that the government sought to alter its relationship with the coalition, and to re-establish and maintain control of the direction of implementation activities. To some, it seemed almost as though government felt that 'enough was enough—time to revert back to previous ways of doing business'. Indeed, it seems evident that the implementation process has been hampered by ongoing tensions between government and the community coalition in relation to partnership issues. Moreover, there was not enough political commitment to maintaining a truly equal government-community partnership throughout the implementation process.

### Sustaining community momentum
Following the passage of the legislation, the community's energy began to dissipate. After dedicating scores of volunteer hours to the legislative drafting process, many of the coalition's most active members were spent and needed a break. The coalition needed to find ways to recharge itself in order to take on the serious and time-consuming work of implementation. A related challenge facing the community was the fact that by 1993 PRAG's independent funding from the Law Foundation and the Notary Foundation was running out. Lack of funding would affect the community's efforts to retain ownership of the guardianship reform process during implementation. The community coali-

tion would need to either find a new funding source, or solicit government funding to sustain itself (i.e., its independent office). In the end, short-term funding to support the staffing and operation of the community coalition office did come from the government's implementation budget. Nevertheless, issues surrounding the source and terms of ongoing funding had a significant bearing on the sustainability of community engagement processes.

### The champions quit the scene

From 1991 till the passage of the new guardianship legislation, it was clear that the community had an ardent and powerful champion: at numerous points, the BC attorney general, Colin Gabelmann, demonstrated his strong and unwavering support for both the legislative package and the community's involvement in its development. As well, the BC Public Trustee, Myrna Hall, had been instrumental in spearheading the development of the legislation and the government's partnership with the community coalition. She was a keen advocate of the new legislation and she was also committed to revamping the Office of the Public Guardian and Trustee. By 1994–5, however, both Gabelmann and Hall had left their senior posts within the Ministry of the Attorney General. They were no longer in positions in which they could directly oversee or control the implementation and proclamation processes. Gabelmann's successor as attorney general, Ujjal Dosangh, and Hall's successor as public trustee, Dot Ewen, have not provided us with evidence that the legislation's proclamation is a high priority, though both outwardly seem to support it. What seems to be missing is the sense of personal commitment and passion that Gabelmann and Hall brought to the process. It seems as though the work of key individuals as champions of the legislation is essential to successful implementation, particularly when political commitment to the content of the package and to 'equal partnerships' with community may be on the wane.

### The price tag

Finally, the anticipated cost of the legislation must be mentioned, as this is now cited as the primary reason for the delay in proclamation. A discussion about cost is somewhat perplexing, however, since:

a) to my knowledge, in 1993/4 the cost of implementing the new legislative package had been estimated at $3-5 million, yet the provincial government had committed itself to setting aside these funds;

b) by 1996 the government's estimated cost of implementing the package had jumped to well over $10 million—prompting the government to undertake a review of all four Acts associated with the adult guardianship legislation (the stated objective of this review was to find the most cost-effective plan for implementation, and/or to determine whether and how the package could be partially proclaimed, while still upholding the principles of the legislation); and

c) there does not appear to be agreement between the community coalition and government about this $10 million estimate; the coalition believes that implementation costs could be substantially lower than those indicated by government. Indeed, the community coalition has argued that key facets of the legislative package, most notably the Representation Agreement Act, will lower costs to government in the long run, because of the reduced need for public guardianship.

Nevertheless, as of winter 1998, the findings and recommendations of the 1996 review have not been made public, and none of the four Acts comprising the adult guardianship legislation has been proclaimed. Adults requiring decision-making assistance and/or guardianship, their families and caregivers, health and human service providers, and policy-makers continue to operate under existing guardianship laws, and frustration with these laws continues to mount. Further examination and analysis of the (non)-implementation process certainly is warranted, as this chapter has been able to touch on only some of the key issues. However, this story of BC's adult guardianship legislation, which ended its initial phase in July 1993 on such a high note, and which now seems to be concluding its second phase in a far more dreary and desultory way, is perhaps better recast as a tale of *two* processes: 'It was the best of. . . .'

## Personal Reflections

My involvement in the adult guardianship reform process began in the fall of 1991; I was one of the 3,000 people in British Columbia who took part in PRAG's consultation process. Having moved to British Columbia from Ontario the year before, and having recently worked there as a psychologist in an innovative multi-disciplinary clinic focusing on the assessment of capacity, I was extremely interested in BC's emerging law reform initiative and in the processes through which it was taking shape.

Later in the fall of 1991, I attended another large, community-based forum in Victoria sponsored by the Joint Working Committee, during which the Framework Document was presented and participants had opportunities to provide feedback and suggestions for its refinement. The atmosphere at this meeting was open, and members of the Joint Working Committee and PRAG staff genuinely welcomed the involvement of newcomers to the guardianship reform process. Following the forum, I introduced myself to members of the Joint Working Committee and indicated my interest in becoming involved in PRAG's task groups, particularly the one dealing with issues surrounding the assessment of capacity.

PRAG staff forwarded my name to a Guardianship Committee meeting of the whole (along with the names of others who had indicated their interest in participating in these committees), and by late fall I was appointed a member of the Office of the Public Guardian and Trustee policy group.[1] During the fall I was commissioned to co-author (in collaboration with a former colleague from Ontario who had also moved to BC) a position paper on capability and needs reviews, which would be used to support the work of the Capacity and Needs Policy Group. Finally, in the spring of 1993 I was asked to serve as one member of a two-person Legislative Response Committee that was responsible for reviewing the draft version of the Office of the Public Guardian and Trustee Act.

To provide a personal debriefing and to capture my experience of participation in legislative reform work and in government-community partnerships, during the spring of 1993 I kept a journal containing my observations of the Office of the Public Guardian and Trustee (OGPT) policy group process. A summary of my reflections on the experience of involvement in guardianship reform is based largely on these field notes. A number of positive experiences emerged during the process and two of these are described first.

### 1. Citizenship, ownership, and powerfulness

Unquestionably, citizens and groups had unprecedented opportunities to contribute to the framing and even the drafting of the new adult guardianship legislation. The level and nature of 'partnership' with government, and support from key government players (e.g., the attorney general, Colin Gabelmann) was unparalleled.

Needless to say, witnessing the ways in which discussions in our committees at times translated into actual legislative change was highly gratifying. It confirmed that our work—the countless hours spent researching, reflecting, discussing and debating—truly made a difference. For example, as a member of the OPGT Policy Committee and the OPGT Legislative Review Committee, I can link specific sections of the Office of the Public Guardian and Trustee Act and relevant policy guidelines to particular discussions that took place over the course of our meetings. Were it not for our input and deliberations, those sections might have looked very different or might have been omitted altogether. In short, as a citizen, participating in and contributing to the drafting of the adult guardianship legislation led to an emotional 'high' and to feelings of powerfulness. Participation also engendered a strong sense of citizenship, ownership, and commitment to both the process and the product.

### 2. Community and coalition-building

Participating in legislative reform through the Project to Review Adult Guardianship also gave rise to a sense of community and connectedness with others. As participants of PRAG, we appreciated that we were not only working as individuals toward the goal of reform, we were also working together as members of a coalition that was bolstered by its size and diversity. In other words, over the course of three years, our work toward legislative reform not only resulted in new legislation, but it also resulted in the formation and strengthening of a community-based coalition: a coalition that recognized and celebrated its legitimacy, voice, effectiveness—indeed, its power—as a change agent within government. Without doubt, being part of this community greatly enhanced my experience and my learning with regard to legislative reform.

Along with these positive facets of participating in adult guardianship reform came feelings of ambivalence. These feelings stemmed not so much from the work itself, but from aspects of the process of working 'in partnership' with government. The partnership, as noted above, was uncharted. Not surprisingly, people had differing views and expectations about what the relationship meant or involved and how it would function; also not surprisingly, these differing expectations and beliefs sometimes gave rise to feelings of frustration about the partnership and about the reform experience.

### 1. Co-creation vs. consultation: What's the (hidden) agenda here?

For many PRAG participants, the crux of this frustration had to do with the nature of the model that seemed to underpin the partnership between government and community: Were community members working in tandem with government to *co-create* the new adult guardianship legislation, or was government *consulting* with the community in order to get feedback on a preconceived framework for legislation and policy? Taking the latter model one cynical step further, were community members being asked to participate in the reform enterprise just so that government could claim it had successfully undertaken a consultation exercise—and were community participants therefore being co-opted through this process?

As has been discussed above and as Etmanski (1992) has emphasized, participants of PRAG came to the legislative review process with the view that the community had initiated guardianship reform. From this followed an expectation that the community would be co-creating the new Acts and related policy, along with government. Therefore, working with government meant (or *should* mean) sitting down to jointly develop a framework—starting with blank paper, so to speak—and being guided by community members' perspectives and experiences with the existing legislation.

For the most part, a co-creation model did guide the framing of the new legislation. However, by 1993, several years after the process began, it seemed that many influential government participants in the reform process were interested in something more akin to a consultative approach to working with community. Indeed, sitting as a member of the joint OPGT policy committee, it was clear to me that for many government participants, 'partnership' did not follow a co-creation model. Instead, partnership with community meant working with community 'advisers' who would provide feedback on the government's conceptualization and drafts of the new legislation. This occurred in the OPGT policy group, where fully developed models, diagrams, and organizational charts—documents which had been carefully prepared and presented in a highly polished way—were presented to community participants. Hence, given our unwavering expectation of a co-creation model of partnership, the process guiding the OPGT policy committee often felt frustrating. As I observed regarding the OPGT policy group process:

> It's the process that doesn't really sit well. . . . We cannot pretend that this is true community or citizen participation. Not in the sense that we are participating to jointly develop a model. No, we are being asked to endorse a model that has had months to evolve in the Public Trustee's Office. . . . The process does not take advantage of our strengths and skills. It does not value or acknowledge our beliefs and experiences with the system. We are forced to fit within the government's paradigm for 'community participation', without their understanding that for us, that paradigm has shifted. (Journal entry, 12 March 1993)

### 2. Partnership process: Just how 'equal' are we?

Another related source of frustration for community members of the joint policy groups was the feeling that government and community were not, in fact, equal partners. Again, it is possible that earlier in the reform process the power dynamics were more balanced, and that the issue of power, and power struggles, became more salient as the reform process unfolded and the community continued to demand equal participation. Nevertheless, by the time the joint policy committees got underway, tensions surfaced in relation to the equality of the partnership, and at times, these strains were felt acutely.

With regard to the OPGT Policy Committee, the power imbalance was manifested in a number of ways. First, the OPGT policy group was chaired by the Public Trustee herself (a strong-minded, dynamic woman who had definite ideas about her vision for the new legislation, related policy, and the organization of the Public Guardian and Trustee's Office), and without doubt, the chair exerted considerable influence on the committee's process. Second, community members on the committee were largely dependent on government for relevant information. Yet, as I observed in my field notes, it often felt as though the information we received was selective, and/or that we had scant time in which to absorb it or to examine it critically:

> We are at a disadvantage with regard to a knowledge base. We're reliant on the Public Trustee's Office for our information, and we have little time to properly digest the information we are fed. We are not in the position to evaluate or challenge the information or get a second opinion. Overwhelmed and under time pressure, our responses often feel and sound inadequate. . . . (Journal entry, 12 March 1993)

Third, power dynamics played themselves out in that there was an imbalance in the resources that each 'side' had at its command. The government had ample administrative support, and government representatives served on the committee as part of their regular job. By contrast, for community representatives, involvement with the committee was a volunteer endeavour. Indeed, not only were community representatives not paid to participate in the process, they often had to alter their work schedules or sometimes work

overtime in order to compensate employers for lost time in order to participate in meetings.

These feelings of frustration in relation to power dynamics are discussed
in some detail in my journal, following what was to have been the final Policy
Committee meeting:

> *Theoretically, the last of the OPGT Policy Committee meetings. Clearly, not enough time
> to get through everything. At times, there's a sense that we're making headway—a new
> breakthrough or way of approaching an issue. However, the process continues to be adver-
> sarial on many occasions.*
>
> *The Public Trustee is strained, fatigued. She shows it by being impatient, withdrawing
> from the discussion. She's clearly covered all this ground before and is wedded to many of
> her proposed structures and models.*
>
> *The problem is the mismatch in information, time, and resources that each side (gov-
> ernment and community) has to bring to the discussion. I am frustrated and increasing-
> ly resentful that I don't have the same information to work with as do the government
> members of the Committee. It slows us down: We (the more vocal community members
> of the Committee) need to challenge, to ask for clarifications, to go over 'old' ground
> because we haven't been privy to the same materials as the Public Trustee and her staff.
> We won't rubber-stamp things. But the government is impatient with the time we take
> to process all of the information that is hurled our way. They do not recognize that
> they've had time to live and breathe this stuff for weeks. In the end, the mismatch of
> resources and information makes for a more frustrating and less productive process than
> could have existed, had resources been shared more equitably.*
>
> *Our message is increasingly coherent, however. The focus on public participation in the
> operation, accountability, and evaluation process; the emphasis on returning to core and ser-
> vice delivery values and principles as means to measure effectiveness and quality; and the
> need for accountability mechanisms. I only hope that these messages are reflected in policy
> and legislation. They are ideas that we won't give up.* (Journal entry, 19 March 1993)

These reflections touch on a number of issues that are likely to affect the
contributions that policy communities can make to policy-making in the
human services. These issues are discussed next as they pertain to this experience; however, they have broader implications as well.

### 1. PRAG as a claims-making body

From the outset, PRAG demanded a place at the table as a legitimate partner
in legislative reform; indeed, PRAG was arguably the initiating partner in the
reform process. Moreover, the community-building nature of PRAG resulted
in an emergent self-identity as a coalition, which in turn led to a sense of entitlement within the claims-making process. This sense of entitlement translated into everyday behaviour as: a) PRAG's rejection of having an 'advisory' status and its insistence that the work of community groups be folded into decision-making processes; b) PRAG's use of the political process to access funds

for implementation projects—funds to which PRAG felt itself entitled; and c) PRAG's unremitting concern about decision-making structures and processes in relation to policy development and implementation activities.

Where did PRAG's expectation of being an equal partner in the legislative reform process come from? While we cannot know for certain, the following factors likely came into play:

a) There was a deep conviction among 'founding' PRAG members that the community participants forming the coalition were the most knowledgeable and had the greatest expertise about the need and direction for reform. In other words, PRAG was committed to a 'bottom-up' policy development process.

b) Several of the leading groups within the coalition, e.g., the B.C. Association for Community Living, were organizations with demonstrated strength and tenacity; their legitimacy had already been established with government via previous advocacy and consultation work.

c) Internationally, the strength and momentum of advocacy and self-advocacy movements had been growing for at least a decade, especially among people with developmental disabilities and their families/ caregivers.

d) Finally, given the diverse constituencies affected by guardianship legislation—and given the fact that any of us *could be* affected—society sanctioned and even encouraged citizens affected by the legislation to articulate their needs and vision for reform. Indeed, while the need for guardianship may be stigmatizing, those affected by guardianship legislation are not blamed for their situations. This is in contrast with people on welfare, who frequently are blamed for their poverty and are not generally seen as valued partners in policy reform.

## 2. Resourcing and sustaining the community coalition

Arguably, PRAG's receipt of independent funding through the Law Foundation and the Notary Foundation was instrumental in its success within the legislative reform process. The importance of independent, multi-year funding to sustain community engagement activities cannot be understated. In PRAG's case, this funding enabled the coalition not only to establish but also to maintain a locus of activity—a home base—as well as dedicated staffing, resources for self-advocates' networking and coalition-building, and participatory research. The funding meant that at least some portion of PRAG's work was remunerated, which was significant given that so much of community consultation and engagement work is performed on a volunteer basis. Moreover, the fact that PRAG's funding came from non-government sources was especially important; this provided PRAG with a greater sense of autonomy, particularly at the beginning of the reform process when PRAG needed to establish itself with its multiple and diverse community constituencies. Finally, the fact that PRAG was able to garner multi-year funding, from 1989 to 1993, distinguished it from so many other 'vision and vanish' community engagement processes. Key players within PRAG clearly appreciated the importance of securing an ongoing funding base to extend the work of the community coalition into the implementation phase.

### 3. Who is/represents the 'community'? Where do human service professionals fit in?

As generally occurs in community initiatives, the question of who constitutes 'community' surfaced numerous times over the course of the legislative reform process. The crux of the issue was how human service workers fit in: while not belonging to the government 'side', not all of the community constituencies readily embraced professionals within the community coalition. Distrust of human service workers and disdain for human service models and systems ran high at times among some PRAG participants, particularly among those who argued, echoing John McKnight, that 'you can't have strong communities *and* strong systems—the stronger the social service system, the weaker the community' (McKnight, 1995, p. 43). Ironically, the flip side of this issue—the 'professionalization' of PRAG's community 'leaders'—also emerged over the course of the legislative review process. That is, concerns were expressed that community leaders had interacted so much with government that they no longer addressed issues from a community standpoint.

The perspective of human service workers clearly was not the same as that of self-advocates and/or their families, nor could it be, given workers' experiences and standpoints. Yet, for their part, human service workers rightfully argued that they had valuable contributions to make regarding law reform, and community-based workers identified themselves as legitimate members of the coalition. In the end, a number of human service professionals became active participants of PRAG, and they continue to contribute to various implementation activities and projects. Nevertheless, addressing and resolving this issue was hard work, and required PRAG to uphold its commitment to diversity within the community coalition.

### Addendum

#### Overview of BC's adult guardianship legislation

Embedded in, and at the core of, the new legislative package are five critical principles:

1. All adults are entitled to self-determination: adults may live in the manner they wish; they may refuse support or protection, as long as they are capable and are not causing harm to others;
2. All adults are entitled to receive the most effective, but least intrusive and restrictive, form of assistance;
3. All adults are entitled to the legal presumption that they are capable of making decisions and, where necessary, to support and assistance in order to understand and make informed decisions on their own behalf;

4. The use of court procedures and court orders appointing decision-makers should occur only as an absolute last resort and only after alternatives have been attempted or carefully considered; and

5. All procedures, protocols, etc., should be intellectually, physically, financially, and culturally accessible and appropriate to all adults.

It should be recalled that these principles stemmed from PRAG's initial consultation process; the guiding principles for the new legislation were essentially unchanged from those presented in the Framework Document, *How Can We Help?*. These principles also form the basis of the Acts' implementation, and of the evaluation of the legislative package.

Four separate but related Acts comprise the legislative package known as the Adult Guardianship legislation. These are:

1. The Representation Agreement Act
2. The Health Care Consent and Admissions to Facility Act
3. The Adult Guardianship Act
4. The Office of the Public Guardian and Trustee Act

The Representation Agreement Act sets out what a representation agreement is; who can make one; what kinds of decisions a representative can make or assist an adult to make; and the safeguards that must be in place in order to process and uphold these agreements. In contrast to an enduring power of attorney, which only pertains to legal and financial decision-making, a representation agreement covers all aspects of decision-making in a person's life. That is, representation agreements enable an adult to authorize someone to either help with decision-making or make substitute decisions around personal care, health care, finances, or legal matters.

Everyone is presumed to be capable of entering into a representation agreement. Indeed, there are no tests of capacity prior to making the agreement, although there can be challenges regarding capacity after the agreement has been made. Representatives are obligated to follow an adult's pre-expressed wishes and to involve the adult in decision-making. In these ways, representation agreements are viewed as the legal recognition of an individual's informal support network and as a means to respect and encourage self-determination.

The Health Care Consent and Admissions to Facility Act focuses on the steps that must take place to ensure that an adult or his/her substitute decision-maker has provided informed consent prior to receiving major or minor health care or placement in a licensed facility. The Act also begins with a presumption of the adult's capability. If the adult is found to be incapable of decision-making, however, the Act speaks to the process of appointing a (temporary) substitute decision-maker, outlining the role of the spouse, partner, family, and friends. The Act also sets out the responsibilities of health care providers in assisting people to make decisions about their health and/or personal care.

The Adult Guardianship Act is perhaps the most complex Act within the package; it speaks to issues regarding abuse, neglect, and self-neglect of the adult. The Act provides a mandate for the creation of a community response to abuse and neglect. As well, the Act sets out the procedures that must be followed to obtain substitute decision-making powers on behalf of an adult; in keeping with the guiding principles, the Act stresses that applications for formal guardianship may only be used as a last resort. A critical component of this Act is provision for the review of needs and the assessment of an adult's capacity; that is, the Act separates the process of reviewing for need— the need for decision-making assistance—and the assessment of capability. Finally, unlike previous legislation, this Act recognizes that different levels of assisted decision-making may be necessary; that a person's need for assistance may be specific to a particular area in her/his life; and that the need for assistance may be time-limited and/or that needs may change over time.

The Office of the Public Guardian and Trustee Act provides procedural guidelines that enable the Office of the Public Guardian and Trustee to assume the new duties outlined in the four Acts. Key components of this Act are the establishment of an Advisory Committee to the Office, and a mandatory, independent evaluation of the guardianship system every five years.

# 9

# Community Governance

This chapter examines the potential of community governance to reform the policy process. Community governance brings policy-making and the management of the outcomes of that process to the level of local communities. It is an attractive strategy to many both on the left and on the right of the political spectrum, but this very quality suggests that the concept contains a basic contradiction. Thus, for neoconservatives, community governance means reducing the size and significance of governments by returning the responsibility for helping individuals and families to churches and neighbourhood and charitable organizations. For those who believe in democratic socialism, community governance does not represent an abandonment of state responsibility for the human services, but rather affords the potential of involving more citizens in governance issues. It is a policy direction that replaces the rigidity and cumbersome nature of large bureaucracies with small, user-friendly agencies. While our resolution of this issue will appeal most to those of this political persuasion, we recognize that some on the left favour the centralization of power in the hands of senior policy experts. Our resolution will offend these left-leaning central planners just as thoroughly as it will the neoconservatives.

We begin by describing what we mean by 'community' and 'governance' and then identify both the advantages and disadvantages of community governance. We note some examples and conclude the discussion by presenting our approach to community governance.

## What Do We Mean by 'Community'?

Discussions of community typically begin by attempting to define the term, because of the many different definitions of 'community'. Indeed, forty years ago one author counted ninety-four variations of the term (Hillery, 1957). While 'community' can refer to communities of interest without geographic boundaries, we are concerned here with geography. Thus, 'community' is defined to mean a group of people having common interests and sharing a particular place. But this definition is still imprecise with respect to size since it can refer to neighbourhoods, municipalities, and regions. For our purposes this is not a vexing issue since we argue that the concept of community governance can apply to all of these geographic units. In our view, agencies such

as neighbourhood houses should be controlled by residents of neighbourhoods, while educational, health, and child welfare services should be under
municipal or regional control, albeit with localized service components.

It is important to clarify that our arguments for community governance
do not apply to all health and social policies. Some programs such as income
security and medicare coverage must be provided at provincial or federal levels. Here, the principle of equity is paramount, and equity demands that all
citizens regardless of residence are entitled to the same level of income related to need whether the income is provided through a pension, social assistance, workers' compensation, or employment insurance. We agree with
Piven's trenchant criticism of calls to delegate responsibility for income programs to communities:

> The most serious problems in these programs—of inadequate benefits and
> demeaning treatment of beneficiaries—are surely not likely to be solved by decen-
> tralization or community participation. To me such proposals are exasperating for
> their pig-headed rejection of either history or analysis. No one seems to remem-
> ber the local and private tyranny that bedeviled relief programs for the poor before
> they were at least partially nationalized in the 1930s. (Piven, 1993, p. 69)

Leaving aside medicare and social policies pertaining to income security,
the issue of which services and programs are most appropriately dealt with at
what level is a contentious and slippery one. While it is apparent that the
issue cannot be resolved by unambiguous formulas, some clarity can be
obtained by examining four principles: affinity; affected interests; accessibility; and a low level of bureaucratization.

The *principle of affinity* suggests that people committed to a religious faith
or to cultural traditions have a right to receive services from agencies and
practitioners who are also committed to these values. Examples of the principle of affinity include church-sponsored agencies such as Catholic, Jewish,
and Lutheran family and child service organizations; First Nations agencies;
and ethnic agencies. People coming to these agencies know up-front that
they will receive counselling and other services consistent with their values
and belief systems. 'Affinity is the perception that a provider possesses a
unique set of characteristics which are important to the consumer' (Social
Planning Council of Metropolitan Toronto, 1976, p. 106).

We recognize that some people desiring affinity as a condition of service
will be thinly scattered across wide geographic areas. Hence, affinity may
require municipal or regional auspices where neighbourhood-based services
are impractical or inefficient.

The *principle of affected interests* (Dahl, 1970) holds that those affected by a
decision or a program should have some say in making the decision or shaping the program. This principle has been prominent in the development of
programs and agencies by groups with a particular interest or cause. Some
examples include Associations of Community Living, transition houses,

women's centres, and anti-poverty organizations. And in order for the principle of affected interests to work, the remaining two principles come into play.

The third principle is that of *accessibility*. In his contributions to the Seebohm report on the reorganization of health and social services in the United Kingdom, Roy Parker captured the essence of accessibility by the phrase 'pram-pushing distance' (Report of the Committee on Local Authority and Allied Services, 1968). Such services include day care; meeting places for children, youth, parents, and seniors; and neighbourhood-organizing activities. While the principle of accessibility must be operationalized differently in urban and rural areas, the experience of neighbourhood houses and community schools is that accessibility—both in terms of location and a welcoming, user-friendly philosophy of service—is a determining factor in the use of services. One of the few empirical studies of the effects of decentralization in child welfare demonstrated that accessibility was directly associated with service utilization (McKenzie, 1991):

> To summarize, service demand as reflected by caseload increases in child abuse, family service, and children in care increased at a much higher rate in Winnipeg following the transition to decentralized, community-based services than elsewhere in the province. These data along with the evidence of increased activity in prevention and early intervention demonstrate that regionalization led to significant improvements in child and family services. (McKenzie, 1991, p. 61)

Finally, the *principle of a low level of bureaucratization* calls for a flat rather than a hierarchical structure in organizations. Flat structures provide a hospitable environment for the human services by reducing the number of managerial positions and by providing the potential for a high degree of collaboration between the executive and front line staff.

Our argument is that the more of these principles relate to a particular service, the more local governance there should be. We recognize that some will argue in favour of regional authorities that could delegate service responsibilities to local units. This argument is rejected here on two counts. First, neighbourhoods differ substantially on a number of dimensions and hence should have the capacity to tune programs to their unique needs (Warren, 1981). Second, the regional arrangement returns to the familiar pattern of top-down authority for policy-making, whereas we prefer a bottom-up approach. There are precious few opportunities to delegate the responsibility for policy and planning to neighbourhoods and, hence, when an opportunity is presented, it should be seized.

In order to achieve some economies of scale concerning matters such as purchasing equipment and providing continuing education programs, neighbourhood-based organizations might well form regional associations. But the crucial difference is that these associations would be the creature rather than the master of the neighbourhood agencies. We recognize, too, that many programs require a partnership between senior levels of government and community governance, particularly when substantial funding is required. The nature of the partnerships is dealt with in a later section of this chapter.

## What Do We Mean by 'Governance'?

A number of attempts have been made to clarify the meaning of 'governance' at a community level. Basic to the concept is the delegation of authority and responsibility from senior levels of government that have traditionally been responsible for health and social services. One author distinguishes among political, geographic, and administrative decentralization (Rein, 1972). Geographic decentralization consists of the establishment of local offices without any transfer of power. Political decentralization delegates policy-making authority to the local unit, while administrative decentralization is more restrictive and grants autonomy only with respect to specified tasks.

A more elaborate and better-known framework is the ladder of citizen participation referred to in Chapter 4 (Arnstein, 1969). Arnstein developed the framework in an attempt to clarify the levels of engagement of citizens in the Model Cities programs in the United States in the 1960s. While the ladder refers to citizens rather than communities, the basic intent of the framework—to distinguish between differing levels of control—applies just as clearly to communities as to citizens. It will be clear as the discussion proceeds that our view of community governance involves the top three rungs of the ladder: citizen control, delegated power, and partnership arrangements.

Before proceeding to the discussion of advantages and disadvantages of community governance, we note that neither of the frameworks identified above speak to practice, and in our view a community work approach to practice is an essential component of community governance. The vignette on page 4 of Chapter 1 contains some of the essential components of a community work approach to practice, but it is appropriate at this juncture to describe the approach in a more explicit fashion.

A community work approach to practice contains the following characteristics. The people being served:

a) become partners in developing and managing programs that affect them;
b) become partners in identifying and then taking action to change harmful and negative conditions that are present in their neighbourhood; and
c) have reserved seats at policy-making tables to ensure that not just the professionals and other experienced volunteers participate.

A community work approach to practice is the antithesis of the current and strongly held view in which, in the guise of attempting to co-ordinate services and ensure accountability, people being served are cast as 'cases' and professionals as 'case managers'. This 'solution' has arisen because many individuals are buffeted by problems such as poverty, inadequate housing, unemployment, unsafe neighbourhoods, and difficulties in marital and parent/child relationships. But unlike the interconnectedness of these issues, programs have been developed on a specialized basis and are offered by agencies with specific functions. Since these agencies are often located in different areas, people must traipse from one area to another, and not infrequently they receive different responses to questions and conflicting advice and opinions.

This scenario is described in detail in the first volume of the Gove Inquiry into Child Protection in British Columbia (Report of the Gove Inquiry into Child Protection in British Columbia, 1995). This inquiry made 116 recommendations, and pertinent to this discussion are the recommendations that services should be integrated, provided in a common location, and governed by regional boards of elected citizens; and that a system of case management be developed and implemented. The inquiry concluded that case management is required to ensure that clients do not fall between the cracks of programs and providers.

In our view, the recommendation calling for community governance is sound and progressive, but ironically it is one of the few recommendations that is not being pursued. Being close to and aware of community needs and resources, community governance has the potential to come to grips with this multi-agency problem. Community governance might reduce the number of agencies and thereby the number of service providers involved with any one family; it might organize common sites of operation, and, as a radical innovation, install citizens as the managers or co-managers in the planning and implementation of the services that affect them.

As noted in Chapter 1, we categorically reject the case management strategy. To frame people as 'cases' to be managed dehumanizes them and strips them of their confidence. To put social workers or nurses in the position of 'manager' indicates that they are in control of and can control the lives of the individuals they serve. Such a view is neither feasible nor desirable.

## The Advantages of Community Governance

The case for community governance is summed up in three propositions:

1. People respect more those laws on which they have been consulted;
2. People identify strongly with programs they have helped to plan; and
3. People perform better in projects they have assisted in setting up (Bregha, n.d., p. 3).

Simply put, community governance provides more space for more people to participate, to develop a constituency for the human services, and to increase the sense of participants' self-worth. The advantages have been identified in greater detail by many authors (see, among others, Pateman, 1970; Clague et al., 1984; Cassidy, 1991). They can be enumerated as follows:

1. Community organizations are connected to local customs and traditions. They are intimately aware of the history of issues and of what has been done in the past to resolve these issues.
2. Action on community issues is more likely to be swift if the decisions are made at a local level rather than at senior levels of government.
3. Community governance provides an opportunity for people to learn about the process of governing; thus, it serves as a training ground for engagement in other political arenas.
4. Community governance affords an opportunity for social learning, for individuals to become knowledgeable about social issues and the complex interplay between personal troubles and public issues.
5. Community governance contains the potential for building a constituency for the services being governed. Thus, a constituency for education has been built through citizens participating on regional school boards and parent advisory committees.

All of the above advantages occur because community governing structures are small and accessible. It is easier for citizens to be involved in, to have contact with, and to influence small governing units as opposed to regional and provincial governments. The experience of the Greater London Council, which experimented with various kinds of both functional and geographic structures, was that 'the smaller the unit, the more effective was its attack on hierarchy, fragmentation of services and the deskilling of professional talents' (Murray, 1993, p. 61).

However, the advantages of small governing structures are countered by the claims that they are costly and inefficient. We discuss these claims in the following section.

## The Disadvantages of Community Governance

Earlier, we referred to one significant disadvantage of community governance—the condition of 'acute localitis' (Montgomery, 1979). Acute localitis refers to the potential for communities to become closed and intolerant of diverging patterns of behaviour. While the rural community of old is often romanticized today as a place of support and mutual affection, we often forget that these were also often places of intolerance and even cruelty. As a consequence, many individuals fled to the anonymity of cities, where their views and behaviour were accepted or at least tolerated.

A second disadvantage is that senior levels of government, particularly those of a neoconservative bent, can decentralize responsibilities on the grounds that local communities can do a better job of taking care of people. Offloading responsibility and reducing the resources previously provided for these responsibilities is a favourite strategy of many governments. A 1995 Canadian example of 'downloading' is the elimination of the Canada Assistance Plan along with the Established Programs Financing Act, which had committed the federal government to provide resources to provinces for health, post-secondary education, and income security. The replacement legislation—the Canada Health and Social Transfer Act—transfers responsibilities to the provinces, with a reduction in the share of federal financial support.

Critics of community governance and, indeed, of most forms of participatory democracy often claim that these structures waste time and energy. They argue that they represent yet another layer of government in our already complicated government system. The development of a New Directions policy for health care in British Columbia provides an instructive example of the potency of this argument. This policy was established by an NDP government following a Royal Commission initiated by the previous government. The Commission recommended that funding and the delivery of health services be placed under regional control 'closer to home'. New Directions proposed implementing this reform by establishing regional and community health boards composed of elected citizens. From the outset the policy was hailed by the advocates of community governance as innovative and imaginative. It was also severely criticized by opponents on the grounds that it would create an expensive and bureaucratic form of governance. Attempts to implement New Directions consumed the better part of three years and, in the end, the critics won. Today, no harsher words can be used to destroy a proposal than 'expensive and bureaucratic'!

It is also instructive for this discussion to inquire into the long-standing debate about the amalgamation of municipalities. This debate swirls around the same issues of size, expense, and bureaucracy. Proponents of amalgamation claim that it would reduce the size of the bureaucratic machinery required to run municipalities, thereby reducing costs while preserving the quantity and quality of service. The argument is deceptively simple and appealing: who could possibly object to saving money and eliminating red tape?

Unfortunately for the proponents, the evidence for the consequences of amalgamation does not support the claims of greater efficiency. In a recent and comprehensive review of amalgamation in Canada, Sancton concludes: 'Notwithstanding the hypothetical spreadsheet analyses of numerous Canadian management accountants, the evidence does not support the position that municipal consolidation promotes cost savings' (Sancton, 1997, p. 30).

## Examples of Community Governance

Several examples of community governance come to mind. Voluntary agencies have traditionally been governed by their communities, whether these are geographic or interest communities. Agencies such as transition houses, child sexual abuse centres, Children's Aid Societies, Associations for Community Living, the United Way, and Social Planning Councils are governed by boards of directors. Since the elections of these boards are generally confined to members of the society legally responsible for the agency, and since many members come from the middle- and upper-income classes, charges of élitism are not uncommon. Indeed, some of these agencies have become closed to all but the members of the society and their friends.

Other examples include regional school boards and community health centres. While elections to these agencies can be contested by any citizen, the charge of élitism is still relevant. As we noted earlier, the ability to participate successfully in the electoral process depends on the availability of financial resources and influence, and this tilts the scale heavily in favour of middle- and upper-income earners.

In a very real sense and particularly in small communities, municipal governments can be considered examples of community governance. Voter turnout for municipal elections is lower than for provincial and federal elections, perhaps reflecting a commonly held view that the most important decisions are made by the senior levels of government. Nevertheless, these elections are often hotly contested affairs and the controversial issues of policing, housing, recreation, and zoning that confront municipal councils involve difficult policy decisions. And while cries for the amalgamation of contiguous municipalities and school boards are frequently heard, they are often resisted. In the last analysis, people prefer school divisions or municipal governments that are local, that are more accessible, and that consist of people who are widely known in the community.

## The Effectiveness of Community Governance

The effectiveness of community governance is difficult to establish. The first question is, effective compared to what? Other levels of government? Business corporations? What are the indices of effectiveness? While the effectiveness of the ministries of provincial and federal governments are occasionally evaluated, we rarely venture into the daunting task of an evaluation of an entire government.

Certainly the Children's Aid Societies in Ontario are convinced of the effectiveness of community governance. In a brief to the provincial government, the Ontario Association of Children's Aid Societies stressed the unique characteristics of these agencies: the mobilization of volunteers, the number of innovative programs launched by the societies, and the creation of a province-wide constituency for children (Ontario Association of Children's Aid Societies, 1973). Other successful examples of community governance come from the establishment of Health and Human Resource Centres in British Columbia (Clague et al., 1984), from the regionalization of child welfare services in Manitoba (McKenzie, 1991), and from Shragge's review of alternative service organizations in Montreal. Shragge's conclusions provide an apt summary of the case for community governance:

> The community-based option has shown itself to be responsible and innovative, creating new approaches and service delivery at a level that can respond directly to a range of community needs and problems. One critique of the post-war wel-

fare State centres on its bureaucratic structure, overreliance on professionals, and the fact that planning and control of services are remote from the local community. Clearly, alternative service organizations are able to address these problems even with their chronic underfunding. (Shragge, 1990, p. 153)

Finally, some insights into effectiveness can be gleaned from the studies of well-performing organizations. Building on the work of Peters and Waterman (1982) and a study by the auditor general (1988), Brodtrick (1991) developed a set of criteria that exemplify well-performing organizations in the public sector. These criteria are:

a)  An emphasis on people. People are challenged and developed; they are given power to act and to use their judgement.
b)  Participative leadership. Leadership is not authoritarian but participative whenever possible.
c)  Innovative work styles. Staff reflect on their performance and seek to solve problems creatively.
d)  Strong client orientation. These organizations focus strongly on their clients and derive their satisfaction from serving the client rather than the bureaucracy.
e)  A mindset that seeks optimum performance. People hold values that drive them to seek improvement in their organization's performance (Brodtrick, 1991, pp. 18–19).

While Brodtrick was able to identify a number of federal agencies as well-performing, it is noteworthy that all were branches or divisions within a department. No department as an entity qualified as 'well-performing'. Indeed, we suggest that these criteria would not immediately spring to mind when defining the typical provincial or federal department.

There are many similarities between the characteristics of well-performing organizations and the type of community governance we have in mind. The common characteristics include inclusiveness, valuing individuals, flat rather than steep organizational arrangements, and small in scale and size.

## Toward a Resolution

In our view, community governance is the model of choice for many, although not all, programs. Indeed, a very short program ladder consisting of only three rungs can be identified. The first rung consists of those programs that are purely local and, here, community governance or control should be the rule. The second rung refers to delegated power whereby legislative and resource responsibility is retained at the federal or provincial levels but operating responsibilities are delegated to communities. Child welfare and health services fall on this second rung. The third rung is concerned with programs in which the principle of equity is of fundamental importance. This requires a partnership arrangement between community and senior levels of government. Examples of these programs include social assistance, employment insurance, and pensions for the elderly. Here, community groups and organizations can make an important contribution by evaluating the outcomes of these programs and communicating the results to senior levels of government. Although these organizations will not be primarily responsible for setting policy or delivering services, they provide essential information about the content of these policies and the nature of the services that should be provided.

In conclusion, community governance affords an opportunity to reform the policy process and policy outcomes by involving people who are significantly affected by these outcomes. The following comment puts the point neatly:

> Architects design houses for council tenants according to space standards that they have never had to experience themselves. Transport is planned and run by people who may not travel by bus or subway. Women's lives are planned by men. How often do we hear manual workers explain how services could be run, but shrug their shoulders because they are ordered to operate them inefficiently. The rich knowledge of white and blue collar workers is largely wasted. Japanese management refers to the gold in worker's heads: this is rarely tapped in the public sphere. (Murray, 1993, p. 60)

As we have noted throughout this book, the effectiveness of policy is ultimately determined by the capacity of the local-level delivery unit and the relationships that prevail among staff members and those being served. But efforts to reform the human services usually concentrate on changing structures and rarely on redistributing power from politicians and bureaucrats to service providers and users.

In the last analysis, the resolution of the issue depends on whether one favours the centralization or the dispersal of power. Centralists point to the advantages to be gained from governing structures that enable decisions to be made quickly, with a minimum expenditure of time and energy. They view the work of committees—especially meetings that are long and inconclusive—as a waste of time.

For their part, the proponents of the dispersal of power base their arguments in part on the axiom of Lord Acton—power corrupts and absolute power corrupts absolutely! From this perspective, power-sharing reduces the chances of a few people governing in their own interests and contributes to the development of a more informed and more responsible citizenry. The concern about wasted time and energy is countered by the response that participation is cost-effective because it avoids mistakes in implementation that frequently occur when those who must implement a policy have had no part in its development.

The dilemma is summed up by the observation that 'the real debate is not about cost savings; it is about the nature of local territorially-based communities and about their potential for democratic self-governance within the complex political and economic environment in which we find ourselves' (Sancton, 1997, p. 30). In our view, community governance of the human services represents an essential addition to the limited range of opportunities for citizens to contribute to democratic self-governance. As we have emphasized throughout this book, the representative system of governance is open only to those with the financial resources, the time, and the self-confidence to participate. We have emphasized, too, that the priorities of those individuals who make policy in the human services are vastly different from those who receive the services. Community governance would pave the way for some improvements in an otherwise severely restricted form of democracy.

# 10

## Conclusion

This concluding chapter seeks mainly to summarize some of the key themes developed throughout the book. However, it also argues the case for practitioner/service user alliances, and elaborates on the importance of inclusive policy-making by reference to the literature, in particular to the recent work of scholars Donald Schon and Martin Rein, both of whom have made distinguished contributions to the study of policy-making.

### Toward Inclusiveness in Policy and Practice

The first theme is the importance of inclusiveness to the policy-making process. Throughout the book, but particularly in the chapters on implementation, community governance, shared decision-making, and policy communities, we have argued that attention to the principle of inclusiveness is the single most important reform needed in the human services. It is important because policies that exclude the knowledge of those who receive services and of practitioners will be incomplete and inappropriate. Service users experience the reality of living in poverty and in unsafe neighbourhoods, a reality unknown and foreign to those who have traditionally made policy.

A second and related point is that the inclusive approaches to policy-making we have discussed reinforce and complement each other. For example, vertical-slice policy groups within organizations can provide extremely useful information to community boards and councils, and shared decision-making represents an approach that would be virtually essential in both policy communities and various forms of community governance. All these approaches have in common the determination to enable those affected by issues to have a say in resolving them. We have acknowledged that adding more people makes for an often time-consuming, frustrating, and messy policy process. Nevertheless, in our view 'participation is cost effective through cost avoidance' (Thayer, n.d., p. 19). To repeat once again, taking the time to hear opinions voiced during the policy-making process can avoid the delays and difficulties that often occur in implementation.

While our arguments have been based on experiences in the human services, some supporting evidence comes from the Federal Department of Fisheries and Oceans. At one time a highly respected agency, the department 'has taken a dramatic tumble from grace, lurching from crisis to crisis, while salmon runs plummeted and fishers lost their jobs by the thousands' (Hume, 1996, p. B1). While a number of reasons have been suggested for the department's decline, the most persuasive is the change in management structure: from a decentralized structure that was local and that listened to the views of fishers, to a highly centralized and remote agency located in Ottawa.

We have called for the establishment of policy communities, community governance, and shared decision-making; however, we recognize that their creation requires a substantial, and to date inconsistent, commitment to the principle of inclusiveness. Hence, we do not expect to see large-scale changes in policy-making structures in the near future. Establishing policy groups along the vertical-slice model might be easier to establish, but here again the consent of those in charge is required.

Another strategy—the development of alliances between practitioners and those they serve—clearly represents a formidable challenge since these groups lack both power and resources. However, practitioners and those they serve are becoming increasingly dissatisfied with policy and practice as currently organized. Practitioners are frustrated in their efforts to provide useful and relevant assistance, and, for their part, service users bitterly resent the treatment they often receive at the hands of overworked and overwhelmed practitioners. The potential for action may exist within this discontent.

At first, alliances between practitioners and those being served might not make much of an impact on policies, particularly those in place in large provincial organizations. But such alliances could obtain the backing of other organizations such as poverty groups, professional associations, school boards, and community organizations. Given its anchor in practice and in the realities of the lives of those being served, the work of these alliances would be regarded as real and practical. They could command attention from the media and, at the very least, create some noise that would be substantially more effective than the current waiting-room complaints of staff and service users.

The unique contribution of these alliances would be to change practice since, as noted in Chapter 6, policy reforms typically leave practice untouched. The alliances might focus initial attention on identifying the ingredients of effective practice and might insist that those being served have the responsibility to contribute both to the definition of the issues facing them and to the resolution of these issues. As McKnight observes:

> There is no greater power than the right to define the question. When the capacity to define the problem becomes a professional prerogative, citizens no longer exist. The prerogative removes the citizen as problem definer, much less problem solver. (McKnight, 1995, p. 48)

In addition, effective practice requires a structural analysis and the use of group and community work approaches. Many service users are convinced that they alone are responsible for the difficulties facing them. They lack information about the structural causes of poverty, unemployment, and homelessness in Canadian society. In addition, they typically lack the support of family and friends. Participation in groups with others who are grappling with similar issues enables members to recognize that their situation is not unique nor solely of their own making. Groups can also take action both on matters affecting them and on larger community issues. For example, in the Empowering Women Project identified in Chapter 1, a group of single-parent women took action against the former husband of one of the members. Although forbidden by court order to visit his ex-spouse, the man frequently parked his truck outside her house in an obvious and successful attempt to harass her and the children. The group informed the man in writing that they were aware of his behaviour, that they would monitor his parking, and that they would notify the police of their surveillance. The harassment stopped.

This group also developed a co-operative garden and food exchange that eased their stretched budgets. Co-operative arrangements concerning day care, clothing, and food provide direct benefits and also have an invigorating and empowering effect on participants by providing opportunities to create and contribute. In this way, co-operative efforts go a long way to prevent citizens from becoming clients primarily dependent on others.

Establishing practitioner/service user alliances requires the recognition that these groups have a vital and unique contribution to make. They might begin in a very informal way at the local level, for example, through meetings in neighbourhood homes or at sympathetic community organizations. Indeed, progressive regional managers in provincial ministries or executive directors of Children's Aid Societies can provide modest resources such as office equipment and a part-time staff member to prepare background reports and briefings.

Another version of these alliances might take the form of service user organizations aided by a few key professionals. Certainly, many examples of groups such as the Association for Community Living discussed in Chapter 8 have made important contributions to legislation, policy, and practice. Such groups have prospered in large part because they include a wide spectrum of citizens ranging from working-class people to civic and business leaders. Groups made up solely of recipients of social assistance have enjoyed far less success in changing policies although the National Anti-Poverty Association and some provincial counterparts have struggled valiantly in their quest to gain more adequate benefits and other help for those who require social assistance.

One conspicuously successful example involves the city of Chicago. Funded by the Woods Charitable Foundation, an organization called Women for Economic Security (WES) has established seven chapters and enrolled 350 members from some of the poorest neighbourhoods in Chicago. O'Donnell summarizes the contributions of WES:

> Including clients in the policy-making process seems to have been an essential step in the development of programs that can yield service user-agency co-operation. In the years of Woods Charitable Foundation's investment in participatory welfare policy-making, benefit increases were secured despite the state's

severe fiscal problems, a policy dramatically limiting the 'sanctioning' of welfare recipients (cutting off benefits for apparent failure to comply with rules) was secured, and a workfare program was dramatically redirected from forcing participants into job search programs to encouraging volunteer participation in education programs. (O'Donnell, 1993, p. 634)

It may be unduly optimistic to expect that policy-makers in the human services will declare a moratorium on the policy changes that have preoccupied us to date—changing the geographic boundaries of agencies; integrating organizations into different forms and structures; and creating elaborate arrangements to assess the deficits of 'clients' and to monitor the behaviour of both 'clients' and practitioners. Perhaps if practitioner/service user alliances could get practice right, policy and organizational arrangements would follow quite naturally.

## A New Kind of Professional?

The creation of practitioner/service user alliances and building policy from practice raise the question of whether a new kind of professional is required. Our vision of a practitioner is one who surrenders the desire to control while acknowledging that there are some limits imposed by legislation, by budgets, or, increasingly, by time. These practitioners welcome the contributions of those being served and work hard to establish relationships characterized by partnership, although they recognize that at times the practitioner may have to assume the role of the senior partner.

We struggled to find a role model for the kind of professional we have in mind. In an earlier draft of the chapter we suggested the profession of architecture as a model, on the grounds that at least some architects take seriously the role of consultant in their work with clients. Architects are knowledgeable about construction, about stress factors, and about the pros and cons of various kinds of building materials. But they do not know the specific tastes of their clients with respect to the size of the proposed house, the configuration of rooms, and the personal preference for building materials and interior design. The best results occur when the knowledge and experience of both architect and client are harmonized. However, in reflecting on this suggested role model, we took account of Murray's observation noted in the chapter on community governance that 'architects design houses for council tenants according to space standards that they have never had to experience themselves' (Murray, 1993, p. 60).

In fact, it becomes clear that the closest approximation to our desired model lies within the profession of social work, particularly in the heritage charted by community organization. We recognize that there are examples of community organizers who have aspired to the role of expert, whether as a social planner or community therapist. Certainly one can find support for these roles in the literature of community organization, and Kahn's (1969) early work in social planning and the expert agent of community change described by Lippitt, Watson, and Westley (1958) come to mind. But such works are in the minority: the bulk of the literature in community organization and the majority of practitioners in the field exemplify the respectful, 'consumer'-centred professional. Achieving partnerships among those involved in the human services will not be easy, particularly since some who receive service may not choose a partnership model or may have few supports to assist in operationalizing such an approach. But the difficulties should not destroy the potential for the partnership. The kind of professional we have in mind, then, is characterized by the following attributes:

a) listens and incorporates into practice the experience of those being served;
b) respects those being served and treats them as citizens;
c) provides relevant information and research;
d) analyses information and the pros and cons of various alternatives to resolving issues;
e) communicates in plain language both in speaking and in writing;
f) prepares draft reports for discussion and summary reports at closure;
g) organizes meetings at times and locations convenient to all;
h) chairs meetings when appropriate;
i) ensures that all affected have the chance to participate and to provide leadership; and
j) has thorough knowledge of the community and of the issues facing those with whom he/she works.

Professionals do have unique and specific knowledge and skills. They know other professionals; they are aware (or should be) of power and how it is unequally distributed in Canadian society; they are cognizant of insights based on research and studies of change in other jurisdictions; and they are knowledgeable about their domain of practice, whether in the sphere of policy or direct practice. Thus, policy professionals know about the policy-making process, the preferences of the government in power, and the context of the budget and resources available, and this information must be communicated in a respectful fashion to those being served.

A useful insight into the relationship between professionals and those they serve emerged from the efforts of a social action group in Toronto known as the Just Society Movement. This movement was composed mainly of poor people, and the involvement of professionals was allowed only on terms laid down by the activists. Care was taken to sort out the relationship to ensure that professionals did not dominate the organization. A condition for participation by professionals was 'a personal commitment to action and change as a base from which one could then contribute personal skills, insight and knowledge' (Buchbinder, 1979, p. 147). Most importantly, the relationship between the two could not be a 'professional' relationship.

Pertinent to this discussion is the experience of professionals who worked with the Women for Economic Security organization noted above. Only a few were able to relinquish their roles as experts and to function as facilitators for groups of women who met to identify their issues and plan their responses.

Our view of this distinct role for professionals in the human services is similar to the conceptualization of the policy-practice role in social work, a role that has received increased attention in recent years. The policy-practice role is described in the following terms:

> Policy-practice in social work is an approach in which social policy and direct social work practice are combined. It is practised by front-line social workers or supervisors in either public or private settings. Requisite to policy-practice behaviour is the requirement that direct service practitioners, including supervisors, understand and analyse the effects of extant social policy on clients and participate in the modification of social policy that is harmful to clients. These behaviours are operationalized at several levels: the personal, the organizational and the legislative. (Wyers, 1991, p. 246)

Some social work educators have argued that the policy-practice role is so important that it should be recognized as a distinct and new role in social work (Jansson, 1994). While we agree with the importance attached to these functions, creating a new role is not necessarily the answer. In our view, these responsibilities are part and parcel of all front-line practice positions and of all policy professionals. Creating a new role opens up the possibility of letting both practitioners and policy-makers neglect the task of developing inclusive policy-making structures and processes.

A second useful source from the literature is provided by the work of Schon and Rein. These scholars have written extensively on the notion of framing and reframing policies. Their most recent co-publication is *Frame Reflection: Toward the Resolution of Intractable Policy Controversies* (1994); it is impossible to do justice here to the authors' often abstract but intriguing account of resolving policy controversies. However, their primary contention echoes the argument noted throughout this book—that policies are framed by the ideologies and experiences of those who participate in the policy-making process. Since these ideologies often conflict, especially in the most vexing policy matters, resolution is always difficult and often unsatisfactory. Schon and Rein suggest that tackling these dilemmas requires that all the people involved in the process reflect on their own and others' constructions of the problem at hand. In addition, 'frame reflection' requires 'a triadic relationship of research, policy and practice' (Schon and Rein, 1994, p. 197). The triad is necessary because policy-makers are simply too busy and too removed from practice to engage in reflection; researchers lack sufficient knowledge of the realities of the policy-practice connections; and practitioners, while knowledgeable, lack influence and power.

Schon and Rein (1994) sum up the requirements for frame reflection in the following way:

a) civitas—the disposition to try to solve the 'Governor's problem';[1]
b) the ability to contribute to the creation and maintenance of a climate of mutual trust among policy inquirers;
c) the ability to put yourself in the other party's shoes—to discover where they are coming from—in personal and institutional terms, including especially the action frames that shape their interests;
d) the possession of double vision—the ability to act from a frame while cultivating the awareness of alternative frames;
e) appreciation of the necessarily political character of policy design without the cynicism that often attaches to such an appreciation; and
f) the skill of inventing new policy modifications and practices with an eye to resolving frame conflicts (Schon and Rein, 1994, p. 207).

Some differences and similarities between *Frame Reflection* and this book are obvious. *Frame Reflection* includes researchers/academics as members of the triad, but excludes those who receive service. We have noted an important role for research in policy-making, and as Schon and Rein remind us, researchers are often in a unique position to reflect on framing issues as well as analysing and evaluating outcomes. Indeed, the principle of inclusiveness applies just as well to researchers as to other groups. However, we believe that the inclusion of service users is crucial, and perhaps the triad should be described as a quartet. While Schon and Rein do not use the term 'policy communities', frame reflection involving a number of actors represents a policy community in action.

## A Concluding Comment

We recognize that our preferred approaches will be dismissed by those who favour a tightly controlled style of decision-making. In this vein, we derive some comfort from the experience of individuals who were involved in attempts by the Greater London Council (GLC) to experiment with various forms of government. As Mackintosh notes:

> One of the strongest lessons of the GLC economic policy was that it was working relations with outside groups and pressure from outsiders that turned general ideas into effective policies (p. 43). . . . Opening up to the outside is not an optional aspect of a progressive developmental state; it is essential to getting things done and to leaving a legacy behind when the government goes. Sustaining changes in turn means remaining open to changing outside pressures; it is always easiest to shut them out. If developmentalism of a progressive kind is not messy and conflict-ridden, it is probably not happening at all. (Mackintosh, 1993, p. 93)

There may be an important lesson for the human services in this example. At one point in our professional careers we embraced a more centralized government organized system for the delivery of human services; however, we have revised this view. While the state must assure the adequacy of social programs to meet the needs of its citizens, federal and provincial ministries are simply too large and cumbersome to take major responsibility for the delivery of health, education, and social services. Service delivery responsibilities are best handled by structures governed by the local community, and in these circumstances it is particularly important that policy-making involve a partnership arrangement between government and local communities. On occasion, this is likely to be messy and controversial, but that is no reason to avoid experimenting with alternative approaches. There has been a renewed interest in alternative service delivery models recently (see Angus Reid Group, 1997 and Ford and Zussman, 1997). Experimentation with these models may produce some valuable lessons in developing human service systems which extend both the rights and responsibilities associated with policy-making to community members, service providers, and service users.

Above all, it is vital that human service organizations be open to the people they serve, to practitioners, and to the citizens of communities in which they are located. It is vital, too, that these organizations recognize that their responsibilities extend beyond helping individuals who come for service and include efforts to obtain their knowledge and insight about the policy process. In a very real way, only service users and practitioners know how policies are being implemented and understand the real effects of these policies. Unless that knowledge is included as an integral and ongoing part of the policy process, the outcomes from policy-making will inevitably fail to respond adequately to the needs of service users.

# APPENDIX
# A Social Policy Analysis of the 1996 Federal Reforms to Unemployment Insurance

KAREN CAMPBELL

## Introduction

Unemployment insurance (UI) has been criticized by the business community since its inception (Townson, 1986) due to the independence it affords workers in making labour market choices. The changes to Unemployment Insurance discussed in this paper were introduced in 1996, and will be fully implemented as of 2001–2. As a package, these changes suggest that business interests are continuing to have an influential role in determining social policy, including the reforms to UI legislation. Based on the first three stages of the general model for policy analysis outlined in Chapter 5, this case study identifies the principles underlying UI reforms introduced in 1996. The paper[1] also evaluates these reforms against selected value criteria, and presents alternatives to current policy. As indicated, the framework is being used to analyse a policy that has been introduced; thus, it represents a *post hoc* approach to policy analysis.

## The New Employment Insurance System

Unemployment insurance provides income support to workers during temporary periods of unemployment or short-term absences due to illnesses and parental leave. It is financed entirely through premiums paid by employers and employees, and is administered by the federal government. In times of a short-fall, the federal government covers the cost of benefits and is paid back, with interest, when the fund achieves a surplus. Since 1994, the fund has generated a sizeable surplus, and Human Resources Development Canada (HRDC) indicated that the accumulated surplus in the EI account had reached more than $12.8 billion by the end of 1997.

In the Human Resources Development Canada guide to the UI changes and accompanying background documents (HRDC, 1995a and 1995b), the UI system was characterized as 'passive' and 'outdated'; changes were required so that it could meet the demands generated by Canada's changing economy. The government's argument was that UI must adapt to meet structural shifts in the marketplace brought about by technological change, as well as new market relationships characterized by a more global economy that includes international trade agreements. It was also argued that structural, long-term unemployment caused by permanent changes (as opposed to cyclical changes) in the economy and labour market are now being experienced in Canada (HRDC, 1995b, p. 2). When a consistently large proportion of the population is unemployed, the costs of UI increase; however, the money available to finance the program decreases. In these circumstances the government can either increase premiums or cover the deficits until the fund again reaches a surplus. The government also claimed that UI lengthened unemployment and encouraged abuse by providing a consistent alternative to labour-market participation. UI undermines job creation, it argued, by taking money away from business enterprises in the form of premiums, and UI acts in an unfair manner by creating inequities through the exclusion of part-time and multi-job workers (HRDC, 1995b).

Changes to Unemployment Insurance—now called Employment Insurance (EI)—have been grouped under two categories: income benefits and unemployment benefits. The following summary provides a brief and simplified synopsis of the key changes (HRDC, 1995a).

### Income Benefits

a)  Eligibility for income benefits is based on the number of *hours worked* (fifteen hours or more) rather than the number of weeks worked. The amount of work necessary for eligibility is also linked to levels of unemployment in the region where the benefits are claimed. This means that part-time and other non-standard workers who work less than fifteen hours a week with one employer are now eligible for coverage.

b)  The calculation of eligible earnings is based on a fixed period of sixteen to twenty weeks, whether or not the employee was working for that entire time period. In other words, if people worked sixteen weeks in an area with low unemployment, their income, which would form the basis for the level of benefits they received, would be averaged over a period of twenty weeks. Claimants receive 55 per cent of their income if they are eligible for benefits.

c)  Claimants who have collected more than twenty weeks of benefits during the past five years are subject to an 'intensity rule', whereby their benefit rate declines by one percentage point for every additional twenty weeks of benefits collected in the past, to a maximum reduction of five percentage points (50 per cent of their income).

d)  Low-income families who currently receive the Child Tax Benefit also receive a family income supplement to their benefits equal to the amount of their Child Tax Benefit.

e) Insurance premiums have been reduced by 7 cents per $100 for employers and 5 cents per $100 for workers.

f) The amount of maximum insurable earnings was reduced to $750 per week, or $39,000 per year in 1996 and is frozen at that rate until the year 2000.

g) The maximum length of a claim has been reduced from fifty to forty-five weeks.

### Employment Benefits

a) The National Employment Service is to be revamped, modernized, and automated to assist in job searches. It now includes a national job registry and is intended to provide employment counselling.

b) Wage subsidies are granted to people facing barriers to re-entering the labour force in order to facilitate work placements with a view to future employment. Subsidies will only continue for employers who demonstrate high re-employment rates for participants in order to reduce employer dependency on such subsidies.

c) Earnings supplements are to be offered to claimants returning to the work force who would otherwise find it difficult to take a lower-paying job.

d) Self-employment assistance will enable claimants to continue to receive income benefits while they establish their own businesses.

e) Job creation partnerships would allow people to work on community projects and gain experience in the labour market while receiving benefits.

f) Skills loans and grants will be offered to claimants to attend school and/or other training programs in order to develop job skills.

As well, the federal government has discontinued payments, either directly or indirectly, for employers to send their employees on training courses, and the responsibility for apprenticeship training, co-operative education programs, and work-place training has been devolved to the provinces.

## Problem Definition: Government Assumptions About Causality and a Critique

### Government Assumptions Underlying Policy Change

The current social policy environment is being highly influenced, and in many ways defined, by powerful corporate interest groups, subscribing to monetarist principles of the labour market and supply-side economics.[2] They advocate the re-establishment of a 'free' market, functioning on the principles of wage and price flexibility, the mobility of capital and labour, and relative market autonomy. The interference of the state through social welfare provisions undermines the labour market's flexibility, thereby inhibiting productivity improvements and international competition. Based on supply-side economic principles, corporate interest groups advocate the deregulation of business and tax cuts to corporate and wealthy classes on the assumption that money will be injected into the economy and wealth will 'trickle down' to the rest of the populace through increased demand for goods and services. The current deficit primacy and balanced-budget-driven trends in public policy design are directly generated by this desire to pull the state out of the market. In fact, Ronald Reagan's budget director has admitted that he 'deliberately used the deficits to paralyse government social spending and "dismantle" federal programs' (Levine, 1996, p. 61). Also informing the current policy environment is the rise in influence of multinational corporations, their commitment to international trade agreements, and the subsequent globalization of capital. The Canadian government is in many ways synchronizing social programs and public policy with those in the United States, in order to remain 'competitive' in the eyes of business.

Consistent with these views '. . . is the tendency to see workers' behaviour as voluntary where individuals freely make rational choices about their work careers, moving, training and earning in response to opportunities in an open labour market' (Butler and Smith, 1983, p. 396). This philosophy leads to three primary assumptions about the nature of unemployment in Canada, and these underlie the reforms to UI legislation.

### 1. Paid leisure is more attractive than paid work
As voluntary, rational actors in the labour market, workers determine how much they work, through weighing direct and indirect benefits of participating or not participating in the formal labour force (income-leisure choice model) (Gunderson and Riddell, 1988, p. 17). Unemployment Insurance has been accused of increasing the unemployment rate and extending the length of unemployment by making 'paid leisure' more attractive than 'paid work'. In other words, income security benefits encourage voluntary joblessness, since recipients are paid not to work. Following this line of analysis, if no form of income insurance existed, workers would see fewer benefits to voluntarily staying out of the labour market, or would do so for shorter periods of time. Thus, unemployment would decrease.

### 2. UI skews the functioning of the labour market
Federal regulations and income support are seen as artificially sustaining unviable industries and impeding the mobility of workers by introducing capital to economically depressed regions and impeding the abilities of the market to function autonomously (Courchene, 1978). Here, UI has been criticized on the grounds that some of its features—notably the regional extended benefits that provide extra assistance to claimants who live in areas of high unemployment—have skewed the labour market (Torjman, 1994, p. 1). For example, the chronic unemployment experienced in the Atlantic provinces would be averted and/or controlled if such benefits did not exist, since work-

ers would move to regions where there were more jobs (May and Hollett, 1995). This line of criticism maintains that UI is actually creating and sustaining high unemployment in the Atlantic region by encouraging workers to stay in such an economically depressed area.

### 3. The inability of workers to adapt to changes in the labour market is the major cause of unemployment

The current changes embodied in the EI legislation focus upon the 'lack of fit' of worker skills and abilities to the opportunities presented by the market. Unemployment, in an open labour market, reflects the individual's failure to be competitive in terms of skills, training, or attitude (Butler and Smith, 1983). Neoclassical labour theory assumes that the wages individuals earn and demand for their labour are mainly defined by the stock of human capital, i.e., the type and level of skills available in the labour pool (Gunderson and Riddell, 1988). The so-called active employment measures introduced in the EI legislation focus almost exclusively on changing workers in order to meet perceived labour market demand.

### Critique

The federal government's analysis that led to changes to UI legislation completely misrepresented the nature of increased unemployment by neglecting the role of business behaviours and the demand side of the labour market. The labelling of current levels of unemployment as structural—'where skills or location of the unemployment are not matched with the characteristics of the job vacancies' (Gunderson and Riddell, 1988, p. 516)—masks the true nature of the problem. In reality, Canada is experiencing chronic demand-deficit unemployment, 'where there is insufficient aggregate demand in the economy to provide jobs' (Gunderson and Riddell, 1988, p. 517). Unemployment cannot be explained solely in terms of the natural abilities, education, training, or previous job experience of individual workers. When these attributes are analysed, their effects are mediated through the influence of the workplace (Butler and Smith, 1983, p. 393). Clearly, it is not a lack of skills that is keeping so many Canadians outside the work force, it is a lack of jobs (Betcherman, 1994; Hargrove, 1996; Janssen, 1995; National Council of Welfare, 1993a, 1994; Osberg, 1994; Swift, 1995; Torjman, 1994). Cures for demand-deficit unemployment 'usually involve macroeconomic policies to increase consumption, investment, exports or government spending' (Gunderson and Riddell, 1988, p. 518). However, reforms to UI represent exactly the opposite strategy—taking money out of the economy by reducing benefits and thus reducing consumption and investment and curtailing government spending on job creation and social welfare. As well, the emphasis on employee flexibility and adaptability to the new labour market falls short when we realize that the opportunities simply do not exist.

Two other problems are minimized by these assumptions. First, not only are there fewer jobs available, but labour market strategy has placed an emphasis on the creation of 'bad' jobs, often at the expense of 'good' jobs. 'Good' jobs are full-time, have a certain level of security, provide a reasonable living wage, and include other benefits such as pension plans and dental benefits. 'Bad' jobs are part-time, minimum- or low-waged; they are often casual assignments or short-term contracts in the non-unionized sector (Muszynski, 1994; Swift, 1995). A second and related problem is that this labour market strategy increases employees' insecurity and compromises their willingness to challenge the abuses of the workplace, including health and safety problems. Workers are characterized as 'lucky to have a job' and the environment of the 'new economy' acts to discipline workers who might otherwise organize or advocate for their rights.

Other assumptions advanced about the nature of unemployment do not hold up to critical examination. The application of an income-leisure choice model assumes unconstrained choice by workers in the number of hours worked (Muszynski, 1994). Again, this fails to consider whether workers have real choices. If jobs are not available, then workers cannot exercise choice as to the amount of time worked. As well, income insurance pays only 50–55 per cent of normal earnings, which does not present an obvious benefit over a regular salary. Paid leisure only becomes a viable choice when the option of paid work is available. It has been argued that UI benefits are responsible for skewing the market by discouraging the mobility of labour. However, an alternative view is that the business community is responsible for the lack of risk-taking and lower levels of mobility among workers. By creating an insecure environment for workers and promoting state withdrawal from income security and other social welfare programs, the business community encourages workers to minimize risks and increase security through such strategies as staying near family and lessening their financial exposure through lower investment in luxury items and services. 'From the point of view of the macro-economy, the major problem is that all of these ways of avoiding individual risk tend to produce a labour market with less mobility and lower long-run productivity growth' (Osberg, 1994, p. 67). If Osberg is correct, then it is not the provision of income security that limits mobility and flexibility in the labour force, but rather the lack of a safety net that encourages workers to 'play it safe'.

## Using Value Criteria to Assess the New Reforms

As discussed throughout this chapter, reforms to UI legislation were based on several debatable assumptions about the functioning of the job market and the nature of unemployment. Value criteria relevant to the assessment of this policy are: adequacy; effectiveness; equity issues; the impact on rights, statuses, and social justice; and the impact on service user self-determination and identity.

### Adequacy
Adequacy is defined as *provision of benefits or services sufficient to meet identified need*. The current EI legislation does not meet this criterion. Changes in the

amount of time an employee needs to work before becoming eligible for benefits have ensured that fewer people are able to qualify for income support. For example, before the changes, eligibility requirements in areas of high unemployment were twelve 15-hour weeks (or 180 hours) of work. Now, the same worker would need to work 420 hours (or twenty-eight 15-hour weeks) to qualify. The reason given for these specific changes was to reduce unfairness in the system, and to enable non-standard workers to qualify for benefits during a time of increased dislocation in the labour market. However, the effect of such changes is that somehow, in an environment of high unemployment, workers need to find *more* work in order to qualify. In early 1996, less than 50 per cent of the officially unemployed could qualify for any UI support at all (CAW/Quebec Council, 1995, p. 25; Hargrove, 1996), and by late 1997 only 37 per cent of Canada's unemployed were receiving EI.

### Effectiveness

The effectiveness of UI reforms would depend upon their success in *aiding unemployed workers to re-enter the labour force at a decent living wage*. As discussed earlier, retraining programs will not be successful unless the government addresses the true nature of labour-market dislocation, most notably the lack of 'good' jobs. Such supply-side solutions tend to blame workers for not 'fitting in' to the new labour situation. In fact, these solutions treat workers' skills like commodities that can be continuously recycled through retraining programs. 'In a world ruled by the market and the unaccountable corporations that dominate it, workers are so many empty bottles that have to be gathered up and rewashed and recycled continually, with many of them being broken up or rejected as inadequate along the way' (Swift, 1995, p. 17). The impact of training tends to be mediated by three sets of factors: the prevailing labour market situation; the type of program itself (whether the program involves real job skills and its attachment to the demand for jobs); and the worker. 'There are limits to how much retraining and other employment development services can be used to achieve self-sufficiency for low-wage, unemployed, or otherwise disadvantaged individuals' (Betcherman, 1994, p. 44). Even when the jobs are available, training is not effective for all people.

### Equity Issues

Different populations in Canada have differing levels of attachment to and opportunities within the labour market. Even in times of low unemployment, women, women with young children, immigrants, visible minority Canadians, Aboriginal peoples, and people with disabilities all face systemic barriers to employment. Lack of jobs is a general problem, but it is compounded by these barriers. The general assumption in reforms to UI is that training and/or job search assistance will help all workers to find jobs. This does not take into account business behaviours such as discriminatory hiring practices that lead to disproportionate rates of unemployment for these groups. The income subsidies available in the EI legislation to disadvantaged workers to develop job skills are a positive step; however, they still address changing workers rather than the systemic barriers in the market.

### The Impact on Rights, Statuses, and Social Justice

Since the British North America Act (1867, s.36.1), it has been accepted that it is the role of the federal government to reduce economic disparities among the provinces and among Canadian citizens. Through the federal government's support of less economically viable regions, the right of Canadians to live and work where they choose is upheld, and persons can continue to subsist in less industrialized or economically viable regions of the country. However, allegiance to monetarist principles of reduced government intervention and the belief that high labour mobility is essential to free market functioning questions these rights. The intensity rule included in the EI legislation is the beginning of this threat, since this rule specifically discriminates against those living in economically disadvantaged areas.

### The Impact on Service User Self-Determination and Identity

Changes to UI legislation are defended on the grounds that they will promote self-reliance, reduced dependence, self-sufficiency, and autonomy. In fact, the reforms do not truly address these issues. In response to global competition in the 'new economy', employers are trying to maximize their flexibility while minimizing their labour cost commitments, operating with a low commitment to their employees and investing little in them (Betcherman, 1994, p. 42). 'There is no other social program (with the possible exception of Medicare) which has done more to strengthen the day-to-day bargaining power of working people than UI, and therefore there is no other program which is more hated by business' (CAW/Quebec Council, 1995, p. 27). Income security means that workers are not dependent upon their employers for their entire economic well-being. It also means that employees have a certain level of independence in relation to the labour market, and that they do not have to take the first low-paying, demeaning job they are offered in order to survive. By decreasing the number of people eligible for income benefits, by lowering the maximum amount of eligible benefits, and by shortening the length of time over which benefits can be received, the government is undermining the autonomy and independence of workers. As well, the intensity rule increases the stigma associated with receiving income support, since workers who have used the system in the past are not able to collect the same level of benefits as other users. Those who need the system the most receive the least.

## Policy Alternatives

Many alternatives or modifications that could save money and make UI more effective have been proposed. The options presented by the business community and corporate interest groups were not the only, nor the most viable, options; they were simply the ones that the government supported. What follows is a brief presentation of alternative proposals affecting both job creation as well as current legislation dealing with Employment Insurance.

1. Early retirement could be offered to EI beneficiaries over 60 years of age and older who have little realistic hope of finding decent jobs before they reach the usual age of retirement. This would not only save money but it would also shield older workers from a demeaning and self-effacing period of rejection from employers in favour of younger, more technologically skilled workers. The character of Willy Loman in Arthur Miller's play *Death of a Salesman* is an excellent example of the psychological effects of the changing labour market upon older workers.

2. Accessible, affordable child care that allows parents of young children, especially single mothers, to work could be provided (Nakamura, Cragg, and Sayers, 1994, p. 53; National Council of Welfare, 1993b). This would remove some of the structural barriers to labour market participation for women, and contribute to self-sufficiency and to higher standards of living for children growing up in poor families. As well, the high labour content of child-care services virtually ensures that hours of employment would rise if child care were expanded, creating new jobs in the process of enabling more women to enter the labour force.

3. The financing formula of EI could be changed in ways that increase incentives to job creation and penalize job reduction. For example, establishments that generate high unemployment should pay higher premiums to the fund. Alternatively, a system could be designed that takes into account the contributions to the nation's Gross Domestic Product (GDP) that firms make when employing workers. This also implies that the financing formula would recognize that a profitable firm that lays off workers diminishes not only its own but also the nation's potential GDP and saddles society with the obligation and expense of providing for workers' basic needs. Unwarranted layoffs could be discouraged by means of an appropriate penalty (Janssen, 1995, p. 12).

4. The issues of the working poor could be properly addressed through such measures as increasing the minimum wage to at least 60 per cent of the industrial average, providing wage subsidies for poor families, and/or instituting a guaranteed annual income for all Canadians. Studies of consumer buying and saving behaviours show that lower-income households and households with more children consume, rather than save, more out of every dollar of income than higher-income households. They also spend relatively more of their income on domestically produced goods and services because they are less able to afford things like imported consumer electronic products, imported new cars, and vacations abroad (Nakamura, Cragg, and Sayers, 1994, p. 54). More money provided to lower-income families or to families with children goes directly into the economy, and thus generates more jobs.

5. Impose penalties, through higher premiums or exit-taxes, on businesses that transfer jobs and wealth to other countries. The federal government

should require a commitment from businesses to invest in the Canadian economy and in their employees.

6. Restructure the tax system, so that corporations and wealthy Canadians pay their fair share. As currently structured, the tax system is quite regressive, particularly because of provisions that allow businesses and wealthy Canadians to avoid or defer taxes. The revenue generated by the government through the collection of back taxes would assist not only in funding social programs, but also in reducing the debt.

## Conclusions

The changes to UI legislation must be understood as part of the government's commitment to monetarist and supply-side economics. These changes effectively reduce the ability of unemployment insurance to meet the needs of many Canadians who are out of work. It has also been suggested that real productivity increases in the Canadian labour market will be hampered by the ideological commitments of employers and government to weakened labour and by rising insecurity (Muszynski, 1994, p. 321). However, the business community may soon discover that their threats of potential impoverishment, intended to keep the labour force frightened and willing to work at substandard wages and jobs, produce an unanticipated effect. Workers are also consumers, and by reducing the purchasing power of consumers through lower wages and less social security, many businesses may find that the market for their goods has declined. This is likely to have a negative impact on economic growth. It is important to remember that the current business/government commitment to neoconservative ideology that supports reduced social provision is simply the position of particular and very powerful interest groups. As suggested by Muszynski (1994), we need to re-educate both the public and the business community that one of the benefits of the welfare state is that it enhances productivity through development of a skilled and healthy labour force; it also keeps labour markets flexible by providing security for workers in the face of technological change, job loss, and labour market adjustment. We must also remind the public that the UI fund has had a surplus during a period of record high unemployment rates. This surplus is coming directly out of lost benefits for the unemployed; moreover, it negates the government's argument that the system is too costly to maintain.

At the same time, EI is only one piece of the package, and 'no amount of tinkering with this system will correct for fundamental flaws in economic policies of federal and provincial governments' (Janssen, 1995, p. 11). The government needs to begin addressing the demand-side of the labour market, and to hold the business community accountable for detrimental behaviours. If government continues to dismantle the welfare state and ignores the need to play a more active role in economic development, it may well trigger a crisis in the Canadian economy.

# Notes

## Chapter 2

1. 'Monetarist policies' refer to actions taken by the central bank, acting on behalf of the national government, to control the money supply. Monetarism is generally associated with neoconservatism (also referred to as neoliberalism) because it is designed to ensure the full play of market forces. The major goal is to control inflation, primarily through adjustments in interest rates. It is argued that if inflation is low, prices will be determined competitively through supply and demand, and in this environment capitalism will flourish. These policies, which have been popular since the mid-1980s in many countries, can be contrasted with Keynesian policies that support government or state intervention, particularly in recessions, to stimulate the economy by injecting demand (e.g., new employment programs or new money) into the system. While Keynesian policies create or sustain employment, they increase the amount of money relative to available goods and services and can increase inflation. Keynesian policies are associated with the development of the welfare state because they support state intervention to modify the free play of market forces in order to redistribute income and opportunities. Monetarist policies generally oppose state intervention or investment, and are less concerned with problems such as high unemployment. Because they are associated with a reduced role for government in managing the economy, these policies also support the expansion of a global economy based on free market principles. According to monetarists, the problem of high unemployment will be addressed as the benefits of new investment, encouraged by low inflation and a free market, increase economic growth and new jobs 'trickle down' to those currently out of work.

2. These percentages add up to 110. The error is in the original source and, hence, cannot be corrected here.

## Chapter 3

1. Strategic planning, as the label implies, reflects the adoption of military jargon, and this is somewhat unfortunate. The term is adopted here advisedly only because it is commonly used to indicate a mid-range approach to planning.

## Chapter 4

1. In 1994, the federal Minister of Human Resources introduced a Green Paper on social security reforms, and a parliamentary committee held public hearings in major centres across the country. However, groups and individuals wishing to make presentations had to apply in advance to be heard, and government staff

and politicians reviewed these applications and selected those who would be allowed to present briefs at these public meetings.

## Chapter 7

1. *Land Use Charter*, Commission on Resources and Environment (CORE) (August 1992), adopted in principle by the BC government in June 1993.

2. See the *Provincial Land Use Strategy*, Volumes 1-4, Commission on Resource and Environment; and *Strategy for Sustainability*, CORE Report to the Legislative Assembly, Commission on Resources and Environment, July 1995.

3. *The Provincial Land Use Strategy*, Volume 3, *Public Participation*, Commission on Resources and Environment, February 1995, p. 22.

4. First described in *Getting to Yes* by Roger Fisher and William Ury (Penguin Books, 1983).

5. *The Provincial Land Use Strategy*, Volume 3, *Public Participation*, Commission on Resources and Environment, February 1995, p. 22.

6. *The Provincial Land Use Strategy*, Volume 3, *Public Participation*, Part 2, 'Community Participation', Commission on Resources and Environment.

## Chapter 8

1. It was fortunate that my work at that time required frequent forays into Vancouver. Otherwise, I wouldn't have been able to participate in the policy group. It is noteworthy also that with the exception of myself in Victoria and another person from Gabriola Island, all community members of the joint policy groups came from the Greater Vancouver area. Government members came from both Victoria and Vancouver; presumably, the travel costs of Victoria-based government committee members were paid by government.

## Chapter 10

1. 'Civitas' is described as a 'disposition to work towards the larger purposes of state government' (Schon and Rein, 1994, p. 180). Thus, trying to solve the 'Governor's problem' refers, in the Canadian context, to a willingness to consider and address the broad purposes of provincial or federal governments.

## Appendix

1. An earlier draft of this paper was completed as an assignment for a graduate level Social Work course on 'The Practice of Planning and Policy Analysis'.

2. This very simplified discussion of these theories was informed by the following: Courchene, 1978; Mishra, 1984; McQuaig, 1991; Ehrenreich, 1987; Muszynski, 1994; and L. Kaminski's summary of economic theories of the free market system in class lectures.

# References

Angus Reid Group (1997). *Alternative Service Delivery—A Final Report*. Toronto: Ernst and Young.

Arnstein, S.R. (1969). 'A Ladder of Citizen Participation', *Journal of the American Institute of Planners* 4, 216–24.

Attridge, C., and M. Callahan (1990). 'Nurses' Perspectives of Quality Work Environments', *Canada's Journal of Nursing Administration* 3 (3), 18–24.

Auditor General of Canada (1988). 'Attributes of Well-Performing Organizations', in *Annual Report*. Ottawa: Author.

Bardach, E. (1977). *The Implementation Game*. Cambridge, Mass. MIT Press.

Berman, P. (1980). 'Thinking About Programmed and Adaptive Implementation', in H. Ingram and D. Mann, eds, *Why Policies Succeed or Fail*, pp. 205–27. Beverly Hills, Calif.: Sage.

Betcherman, G. (1994). 'A Job is the Best Social Policy', in K. Banting and K. Battle, eds, *A New Social Vision for Canada? Perspectives on the Federal Discussion Paper on Social Policy Reform* (pp. 37–46). Ottawa: Caledon Institute of Social Policy.

Boulding, K. (1964). Book review: *A Strategy of Decision* by D. Braybrooke and C. Lindblom, *American Sociological Review* 25 (5), 29.

Bregha, F. (n.d.). *Public Participation in Planning, Policy and Program*. Toronto: Ministry of Community and Social Services.

Brodtrick, O. (1991). 'A Second Look at the Well-Performing Organization', in J. McDavid and B. Marson, eds, *The Well-Performing Organization*, pp. 16–22. Toronto: Institute of Public Administration of Canada.

Bryson, J.M. (1988). *Strategic Planning for Public and Non-profit Organizations: A Guide to Strengthening and Sustaining Organization Achievement*. San Francisco: Jossey-Bass.

Buchbinder, H. (1979). 'The Just Society Movement', in B. Wharf, ed., *Community Work in Canada*, pp. 129–52. Toronto: McClelland and Stewart.

Butler, P.M., and R. Smith (1983). 'The Worker, the Workplace and the Need for Unemployment Insurance', *Canadian Review of Sociology and Anthropology* 20 (4), 393–411.

Callahan, M. (1993). 'Feminist Approaches to Child Welfare', in B. Wharf, ed., *Rethinking Child Welfare*, pp. 172–209. Toronto: McClelland and Stewart.

Callahan, M., and C. Attridge (1990). *Women in Women's Work: Social Workers Talk About Their Work in Child Welfare*. Victoria, BC: School of Social Work, University of Victoria.

Callahan, M., L. Hooper, and B. Wharf (1998). *Protecting Children by Empowering Women: The Nanaimo and Parksville Projects*. Victoria, BC: School of Social Work, University of Victoria.

Callahan, M., and C. Lumb (1995). 'My Cheque or My Children', *Child Welfare* 74 (3), 795–819.

Callahan, M., and B. Wharf (1995). *Strengthening Families Through Empowering Women*. Victoria, BC: School of Social Work, University of Victoria.

Cameron, D., and E. Finn (1996). *10 Deficit Myths: The Truth About Government Debts and Why They Don't Justify Cutbacks*. Ottawa: Canadian Centre for Policy Alternatives.

Cameron, G. (1995). 'The Nature and Effectiveness of Parent Mutual Aid Organizations in Child Welfare', in J. Hudson and B. Galaway, eds, *Child Welfare in Canada*, pp. 66–82. Toronto: Thompson Educational Publishing.

Canadian Centre for Policy Alternatives (1997). *1997 Alternative Federal Budget*. Ottawa: Author.

Carley, M. (1980). *Rational Techniques in Policy Analysis*. London: Heinemann.

Cassidy, F. (1991). 'Organizing for community control', *The Northern Review* 11, 17–34.

CAW/Quebec Council (1996). 'Saving the Safety Net: The Attack on Canada's Social Programs', *Canadian Dimension* 29 (6), 25–32.

Chambers, D.E. (1986). *Social Policy and Social Programs: Method for the Practical Public Policy Analyst*. New York: Macmillan.

Chase, G. (1979). 'Implementing a Human Service Program: How Hard Will It Be?', *Journal of Public Policy* 27 (4).

Clague, M., R. Dill, R. Seebaran, and B. Wharf (1984). *Reforming Human Services: The Experience of the Community Resource Boards in B.C.* Vancouver: University of British Columbia Press.

Clement, W. (1975). *The Canadian Corporate Elite: An Analysis of Economic Power*. Toronto: McClelland and Stewart.

———— (1983). *Class, Power and Property*. Toronto: Methuen.

Cohen, M., J. March, and J. Olsen (1972). 'A Garbage Can Model of Organizational Choice', *Administrative Science Quarterly* 17, 1–25.

Coleman, W., and G. Skogstad, eds (1990). *Policy Communities and Public Policy in Canada*. Toronto: Copp Clark Pittman.

Commission on Resources and Environment (1994). *The Provincial Land Use Strategy (Volume 1: A Sustainability Act for British Columbia)*. Victoria, BC: Queen's Printer.

Commission on Resources and Environment (December 1994). *The Provincial Land Use Strategy (Volume 2: Planning for Sustainability)*. Victoria, BC: Queen's Printer.

Commission on Resources and Environment (February 1995). *The Provincial Land Use Strategy (Volume 3: Public Participation)*. Victoria, BC: Queen's Printer.

Commission on Resources and Environment (February 1995). *The Provincial Land Use Strategy (Volume 4: Dispute Resolution)*. Victoria, BC: Queen's Printer.

Council of Canadians (1997). *Canadian Perspective* (Fall). Ottawa: Author.

Courchene, T.J. (1978). *Regional Adjustment, the Transfer System and Canadian Federalism*. Paper prepared for the Senate Committee on National Finance.

Dahl, R. (1961). *Who Governs? Democracy and Power in an American City*. New Haven: Yale University Press.

——— (1970). *After the Revolution*. New Haven: Yale University Press.

Dobelstein, A.W. (1990). *Social Welfare: Policy and Analysis*. Chicago: Nelson-Hall.

Doern, G.B., and R.W. Phidd (1992). *Canadian Public Policy: Ideas, Structure, Process*. 2nd edn. Scarborough, Ont.: Nelson.

Domhoff, C.W. (1967). *Who Rules America?*. Englewood Cliffs, NJ: Prentice Hall.

——— (1971). *The Higher Circles*. New York: Vintage Books.

Durie, H., and A. Armitage (1996). *Planning for Implementation of B.C.'s Child, Family, and Community Service Act*. Victoria, BC: School of Social Work, University of Victoria.

Ehrenreich, B. (1987). 'The New Right Attack on Social Welfare', in F. Block et al., eds, *The Mean Season: The Attack on the Welfare State*. New York: Pantheon Books.

Elmore, R. (1979a). *Complexity and Control: What Legislators and Administrators Can Do About Implementation*. Seattle: University of Washington Institute of Governmental Research. Public Policy Paper #11.

——— (1979b). 'Organizational Models of Social Program Implementation', *Public Policy* 2 (2), 185–228.

——— (1982). 'Backward Mapping: Implementation Research and Policy Decisions', in W. Williams, ed., *Studying Implementation: Methodological and Administrative Issues*, pp. 18–35. Chatham, NJ: Chatham House.

Etmanski, A. (1992). 'Anatomy of a Community Coalition: Reflections on the Project to Review Adult Guardianship Coalition', *SPARC News* (Summer).

——— (1993). 'Anatomy of a Coalition II', *SPARC News* (Fall), 10–13.

Etzioni, A. (1967). 'Mixed Scanning: A "Third" Approach to Decision-Making', *Public Administration Review* 27, 385–92.

——— (1976). *Social Problems*. Englewood Cliffs, NJ: Prentice-Hall.

Fabricant, M. (1985). 'The Industrialization of Social Work Practice', *Social Work* 30 (5), 389–402.

Fetterman, D., S. Kaftarian, and A. Wanderman, eds (1986). *Empowerment Evaluation*. Thousand Oaks, Calif.: Sage.

Fisher, R., and W. Ury (1983). *Getting to Yes*. Penguin Books.

Flynn, J.P. (1992). *Social Agency Policy*. 2nd edn. Chicago: Nelson-Hall.

Ford, R., and D. Zussman, eds (1997). *Alternative Service Delivery: Sharing Governance in Canada*. Toronto: IPAC and KPMG for Government Foundation.

Frankel, H., B. McKenzie, D. Fuchs, I. Guberman, and S. Taylor-Henley (1996). *An Evaluation of the Family Aide and Family Support Programs at Child and Family Services of Western Manitoba*. Winnipeg: Child and Family Services Research Group, Faculty of Social Work, University of Manitoba.

Fuchs, D. (1995). 'Preserving and Strengthening Families and Protecting Children: Social Network Intervention, a Balanced Approach to the Prevention of Child Maltreatment', in J. Hudson and B. Galaway, eds, *Child Welfare in Canada*, pp. 113–23. Toronto: Thompson Educational Publishing.

Gabelmann, C. (1993). Letter to Bill Trott, Chair, Legislative Response Committee.

Gallagher, J., and R. Haskins (1984). *Policy Analysis*. New York: Ablex.

Galt, V. (1997). 'Ranks of Poor Swell to 16-Year High, Council Finds', *The Globe and Mail*, 5 April, p. A4.

Gil, D.G. (1990). *Unravelling Social Policy*. 4th edn. Rochester, Vt: Schenkman.

*Globe and Mail* (1998). 'Fifty CEOs Who Made Between $27.4 Million and $2.0 Million' and 'Fifty More Who Made Between $1.9 Million and $909,467', 18 April, pp. B6–B7.

Goldstein, H. (1992). 'Should Social Workers Base Practice Decisions on Empirical Research? No', in E. Gambrill and R. Pruger, eds, *Controversial Issues in Social Work*, pp. 107–23. Boston: Allyn & Bacon.

Greider, W. (1992). *Who Will Tell the People: The Betrayal of American Democracy*. New York: Simon & Schuster.

Gunderson, M., and W.C. Riddell (1988). *Labour Market Economics: Theory, Evidence and Social Policy in Canada*. 2nd edn. Toronto: McGraw-Hill Ryerson Ltd.

Gwyn, R. (1995). 'Two Cheers, One Boo for Ontario Cutbacks', *Times Colonist*, 27 July, p. 8.

Hargrove, B. (1996). 'Whose Unemployment-Insurance Surplus Is It, Anyway?', *The Globe and Mail*, 18 March, p. A17.

Hargrove, E. (1975). *The Missing Link: The Study of the Implementation of Social Policy*. Washington, DC: The Urban Institute.

Herman, J., L. Morris, and C. Fitz-Gibbon (1987). *Evaluator's Handbook*. Newbury Park, Calif.: Sage.

Hillery, G. (1957). 'Definitions of Community: Areas of Agreement', *Rural Sociology* 20 (2), 14–23.

Human Resources Development Canada (1995a). *A 21st Century Employment System for Canada: Guide to the Employment Insurance Legislation*. Ottawa: Minister of Supply and Services Canada.

——— (1995b). *Backgrounder 2: The Need for Change*. Ottawa: Author.

Hume, M. (1996). 'DFO, The Decline of a Federal Empire', *Vancouver Sun*, 21 December, p. B1.

Hunter, F. (1963). *Community Power Structure*. Chapel Hill: University of North Carolina Press.

Jansson, B.S. (1994). *Social Policy: From Theory to Policy Practice*. 2nd edn. Belmont, Calif.: Brooks/Cole.

Janssen, W.P. (1995). 'In Support of Real UI Reform', *Canadian Dimension* 29 (2), 11–13.

Jennings, B. (1964). *Community Influentials*. New York: The Free Press of Glencoe.

Kahn, A.J. (1969). *Theory and Practice of Social Planning*. New York: Russell Sage Foundation.

Kingdon, J.K. (1995). *Agendas, Alternatives, and Public Policies*. 2nd edn. New York: HarperCollins.

Kitchen, B., A. Mitchell, P. Clutterbuck, and M. Novick (1991). *Unequal futures*. Toronto: The Child Poverty Action Group and The Social Planning Council of Metropolitan Toronto.

Kouzes, J.M., and P.R. Mico (1979). 'Domain Theory: An Introduction to Organizational Behaviour in Human Service Organizations', *The Journal of Applied Behavioural Science* 15 (4), 449–69.

Labonte, R., and J. Feather (1996). *Handbook on Using Stories in Health Promotion Practice*. Ottawa: Health Canada.

Lapham, L.H. (1988). *Money, Class and Power in America*. New York: Random House.

Levine, R.A. (1996). 'The Economic Consequences of Mr. Clinton', *The Atlantic Monthly* (July), 60–5.

Lind, M. (1995). 'To Have and Have Not. Notes on the Progress of the American Class War', *Harpers*, 290 (1741), 35–49.

Lindblom, C.E. (1959). 'The Science of Muddling Through', *Public Administration Review* 19, 79–88.

——— (1968). *The Policy-Making Process*. Englewood Cliffs, NJ: Prentice-Hall.

——— (1979). 'Still Muddling, Not Yet Through'. *Public Administration Review* 39 (6), 517–26.

Linder, S.H., and B.G. Peters (1987). 'A Design Perspective on Policy Implementation: The Fallacies of Misplaced Prescription', *Policy Studies Review* 61 (3), 459–76.

Lippitt, R., J. Watson, and B. Westley (1958). *The Dynamics of Planned Change*. New York: Harcourt, Brace and World, Inc.

Lipsky, M. (1980). *Street-Level Bureaucracy*. New York: Russell Sage.

Love, A. (1992). 'The Evaluation of Implementation: Case Studies', in J. Hudson, J. Mayne, and R. Thomlison, eds, *Action-Oriented Evaluation in Organizations*, pp. 135–59. Toronto: Wall & Emerson.

Lundberg, F. (1968). *The Rich and the Super Rich*. New York: Bantam Books.

MacBeath, A. (1957). *Can Social Policies be Rationally Tested?* (The L.T. Hobhouse Memorial Trust Lecture). London: Oxford University Press.

McKenzie, B. (1989). *Decentralizing Child Welfare Services: Effects on Service Demand and the Job Morale of Street-Level Bureaucrats*. Doctoral dissertation, Arizona State University, Tempe.

———— (1991). 'Decentralization in Winnipeg: Assessing the Effects of Community-Based Child Welfare Services', *Canadian Review of Social Policy* 27, 57–66.

———— (1994). *Evaluation of the Pilot Project in Block Funding for Child Maintenance*. Winnipeg: West Region Child and Family Services.

———— (1997). 'Developing First Nations Child Welfare Standards: Using Evaluation Research Within a Participatory Framework', *The Canadian Journal of Program Evaluation* 12 (1), 133–48.

McKenzie, B., and I. Guberman (1997). 'For the Sake of the Children: A Program for Separating and Divorcing Parents', *The Social Worker* 65 (3), 107–18.

Mackintosh, M. (1993). 'Creating a Developmental State: Reflections on Policy as Process', in G. Albo, D. Langille, and L. Panitch, eds, *A Different Kind of State? Popular Power and Democratic Administration*, pp. 51–65. Toronto: Oxford University Press.

McKnight, J. (1995). *The Careless Society: Community and Its Counterfeits*. New York: Basic Books.

McKnight, J., and J. Kretzmann (1992). 'Capacity Mapping', *New Design* (Winter) 9–15.

McQuaig, L. (1987). *Behind Closed Doors*. Toronto: Viking.

———— (1991). *The Quick and the Dead*. Toronto: Viking.

———— (1993). *The Wealthy Banker's Wife*. Toronto: Penguin Books.

———— (1995). *Shooting the Hippo*. Toronto: Viking.

Majchrzak, A. (1984). *Methods for Policy Research*. Newbury Park, Calif.: Sage.

Maluccio, A. (1997). *Assessing Child Welfare Outcomes: The North American Perspective*. Presentation to Third International Conference on The Looking After Children Initiative, Oxford, England, 17–18 March.

Marchak, M.P. (1991). *The Integrated Circus: The New Right and the Restructuring of the Global Economy*. Montreal: McGill-Queen's University Press.

Marris, P., and M. Rein (1967). *The Dilemmas of Social Reform*. New York: Russell Sage.

May, D., and A. Hollett (1995). *The Rock in a Hard Place: Atlantic Canada and the UI Trap*. Toronto: C.D. Howe Institute.

Mills, C.W. (1956). *The Power Elite*. New York: Oxford University Press.

———— (1959). *The Sociological Imagination*. London: Oxford University Press.

Mimoto, H., and P. Cross (1991). 'The Growth of the Federal Debt', *Canadian Economic Observer* 4 (6), 3.1–3.18.

Ministry of Social Services (1993). *Making Changes: Next Steps* (A White Paper for Public Review). Victoria, BC: Author.

Ministry of Women's Equality (1994). *The Gender Lens: Policy Analyst Version*. Victoria, BC: Author.

Mintzberg, H. (1983). *Structure in Fives: Designing Effective Organizations*. Englewood Cliff, NJ: Prentice-Hall.

Mishra, R. (1984). *The Welfare State in Crisis: Social Thought and Social Change*. New York: St Martin's Press.

Montgomery, J. (1979). 'The Populist Front in Rural Development: Or Shall We Eliminate Bureaucracies and Get On With the Job', *Public Administration Review* (Jan/Feb), pp. 58–65.

Moroney, R.M. (1991). *Social Policy and Social Work*. New York: Aldine de Gruyter.

Morris, N. (1995). 'Kids at Work', *Maclean's*, 11 December, pp. 28–30.

Morrissette, V., B. McKenzie, and L. Morrissette (1993). 'Towards an Aboriginal Model of Social Work Practice', *Canadian Social Work Review* 10 (1), 91–108.

Mullen, E. (1992). 'Should Social Workers Base Practice Decisions on Empirical Research? Yes', in E. Gambrill and R. Pruger, eds, *Controversial Issues in Social Work*, pp. 107–123. Boston: Allyn & Bacon.

Murray, R. (1993). 'Transforming the "Fordist" State', in G. Albo, D. Langille, and L. Panitch, eds, *A Different Kind of State? Popular Power and Democratic Administration*, pp. 51–65. Toronto: Oxford University Press.

Muszynski, L. (1994). 'Defending the Welfare State and Labour Market Policy', in A. Johnson, S. McBride, and P. Smith, eds, *Continuities and Discontinuities: The Political Economy of Social Welfare and Labour Market Policy in Canada*, pp. 306–26. Toronto: University of Toronto Press.

Nairne, D. (1997). 'Teens Demand Help', *Winnipeg Free Press*, 23 March, p. A1.

Nakamura, A., J. Cragg, and K. Sayers (1994). 'The Employment-Social Security Reform Connection', in K. Banting and K. Battle, eds, *A New Social Vision for Canada? Perspective on the Federal Discussion Paper on Social Policy Reform*, pp. 47–56. Ottawa: Caledon Institute of Social Policy.

Nakamura, R.T. (1987). 'The Textbook Policy Process and Implementation Research', *Policy Studies Review* 7 (1), 142–55.

National Council of Welfare (1994). *A Blueprint for Social Security Reform*. Ottawa: Ministry of Supply and Services Canada.

——— (1993a). *Incentives and Disincentives to Work*. Ottawa: Ministry of Supply and Services Canada.

——— (1993b). *First Thoughts About Reforming Social Programs: Unemployment Insurance and Welfare*. Ottawa: Ministry of Supply and Services Canada.

Newman, P. (1975). *The Canadian Establishment*. Toronto: McClelland and Stewart.

———— (1981). *The Canadian Establishment. Volume II: The Acquisitors.* Toronto: McClelland and Stewart.

O'Donnell, S. (1993). 'Involving Clients in Welfare Policy-Making', *Social Work* 38 (5).

Ontario Association of Children's Aid Societies (1973). '*Brief to the Task Force on Family and Children's Services*'. Unpublished. Toronto: Author.

Osberg, L. (1994). 'Jobs and Growth: The Missing Link', in K. Banting and K. Battle, eds, *A New Social Vision for Canada: Perspective on the Federal Discussion Paper on Social Policy Reform*, pp. 57–69. Ottawa: Caledon Institute of Social Policy.

Owen, B. (1997). 'Hearts Harden Against the Poor', *Winnipeg Free Press*, 24 February, pp. A1–2.

Pal, L.A. (1992). *Public Policy in Canada: An Introduction.* Toronto: McClelland and Stewart.

Panitch, L. (ed.). (1977). *The Canadian State.* Toronto: University of Toronto Press.

Pateman, Carole (1970). *Participation and Democratic Theory.* Cambridge: Cambridge University Press.

Peters, T.J., and R.H. Waterman (1982). *In Search of Excellence.* New York: Warner Books.

Piven, F.F. (1993). 'Reforming the Welfare State: The American Experience', in G. Albo, D. Langille, and L. Panitch, eds, *A Different Lind of State? Popular Power and Democratic Administration*, pp. 66–74. Toronto: Oxford University Press.

Porter, J. (1965). *The Vertical Mosaic: An Analysis of Class and Power in Canada.* Toronto: University of Toronto Press.

Pressman, J., and A. Wildavsky (1973). *Implementation.* Berkeley, Calif.: University of California Press.

Rawls, J. (1971). *A Theory of Justice.* Cambridge, Mass.: Harvard University Press.

Reid, A. (1996). *Shakedown.* Toronto: Doubleday.

Rein, M. (1970). *Social Policy: Issues of Choice and Change.* New York: Random House.

Rein, M. (1972). 'Decentralization and Citizen Participation in Social Services', *Public Administration Review* 32, 687–701.

Report of the Community Panel, Family and Children's Services Legislative Review (1992). *Making Changes: A Place to Start.* Victoria, BC: Ministry of Social Services.

*Report of the Committee on Local Authority and Allied Social Services* (1968). London: Her Majesty's Stationery Office.

Report of the Gove Inquiry into Child Protection (1995). *Matthew's Story.* Victoria, BC: Queen's Printer.

Rice, J., and M. Prince (1983). 'Life of Brian: A Social Policy Legacy', *Perception* 17 (2), 6–9.

Ristock, J., and J. Pennell (1996). *Community Research as Empowerment*. Toronto: Oxford University Press.

Rittel, H.W., and M.W. Webber (1973). 'Dilemmas in a General Theory of Planning, *Policy Sciences* 4, 155–68.

Sabatier, P.A. (1986). 'Top-down and Bottom-up Approaches to Implementation Research: A Critical Analysis and Suggested Synthesis', *Journal of Public Policy* 1 (1), 21–48.

Saleebey, D., ed. (1997). *The Strengths Perspective in Social Work Practice*. 2nd edn. White Plains, NY: Longman.

Saleebey, D. (1990). 'Philosophical Disputes in Social Work: Social Justice Denied', *Journal of Sociology and Social Welfare* 17 (2), 29–40.

Sancton, A. (1997). 'Reducing Costs by Consolidating Municipalities: New Brunswick, Nova Scotia and Ontario', *Canadian Public Administration* 39 (3), 267–90.

Schon, D., and M. Rein (1994). *Frame Reflection: Toward the Resolution of Intractable Policy Controversies*. New York: Basic Books.

Shragge, E. (1990). 'Community-Based Practice: Political Alternatives or New State Forms?', in L. Davies and E. Shragge, eds, *Bureaucracy and Community*, pp. 137–73. Montreal: Black Rose Books.

Smale, G. (1996). *Mapping Change and Innovation*, London: Her Majesty's Stationery Office.

Social Planning Council of Metropolitan Toronto (1976). *In Search of a Framework*. Toronto: Author.

Sower, C., J. Holland, K. Tiedke, and W. Freeman (1957). *Community Involvement: The Webs of Formal and Informal Ties That Make for Action*. Glencoe, Ill.: Free Press.

Spakes, V. (1984). 'Family Impact Analysis as a Framework for Teaching Social Policy', *Journal of Education for Social Work* 20 (1), 59–73.

Statistics Canada (1991). *The Economic Observer*. Ottawa.

Stringer, E. (1996). *Action Research*. Thousand Oaks, Calif.: Sage.

Swift, J. (1995). 'Introduction: The Age of Ailing Expectations', in *Wheel of Fortune*, pp. 1–18. Toronto: Between the Lines.

Swift, K.J. (1995a). *Manufacturing 'Bad Mothers', a Critical Perspective on Child Neglect*. Toronto: University of Toronto Press.

——— (1995b). 'Missing Persons: Women in Child Welfare', *Child Welfare* 74 (3), 486–503.

Teeple, G. (1995). *Globalization and the Decline of Social Reform*. Toronto: Garamond Press.

Thayer, F. (n.d.). *Participation and Liberal Democratic Government*. Unpublished paper prepared for the Committee on Government Productivity Toronto: Government of Ontario.

Titmuss, R. (1968). *Commitment to Welfare*. London: George Allen and Unwin.

———— (1974). *Social Policy*. London: George Allen and Unwin.

Torjman, S. (1994). *Social Programs: Tail or Dog?* Ottawa: Caledon Institute of Social Policy.

Torjman, S., and K. Battle (1995). 'Cutting the Deficit in Child Welfare', *Child Welfare* 74 (3), 459–85.

Townson, M. (1986). *The Threat to Unemployment Insurance*. Ottawa: Canadian Centre for Policy Alternatives.

Warren, D. (1981). 'Support Systems in Different Kinds of Neighbourhoods', in J. Garbarino and S. Holly Stocking, eds, *Protecting Children from Abuse and Neglect*, pp. 61–93. San Francisco: Jossey-Bass.

Weller, F., and B. Wharf (1995). *From Risk Assessment to Family Action Planning*. Victoria, BC: School of Social Work, University of Victoria.

Wharf, B. (1984) *From Initiation to Implementation: The Role of Line Staff in the Policy-Making Process*. Victoria, BC: School of Social Work, University of Victoria.

Wharf, B., and M. Callahan (1984). 'Connecting Policy and Practice', *Canadian Social Work Review*, 30–52.

Wharf Higgins, J.S. (1997). 'Who Participates: Citizen Participation in Health Reform in B.C.', in B. Wharf and M. Clague, eds, *Community Organizing: Canadian Experiences*, pp. 273–302. Toronto: Oxford University Press.

Williams, W. (1980). *The Implementation Perspective*. Berkeley: University of California Press.

Witkin, S.L., and S. Gottschalk (1988). 'Alternative Criteria for Theory Evaluation', *Social Service Review*, 211–24.

Wyers, N.L. (1991). 'Policy-Practice in Social Work: Models and Issues', *Journal of Social Work Education* 27 (3), 241–50.

Yanow, D. (1987). 'Toward a Policy Culture Approach to Implementation', *Policy Studies Review* 7 (1) 103–15.

# Index